WIDOWS OF HIROSHIMA

Widows of Hiroshima

The Life Stories of Nineteen Peasant Wives

Edited by
Mikio Kanda

Translated by
Taeko Midorikawa

St. Martin's Press   New York

© Iwanami Shoten, Publishers 1982

English translation © The Macmillan Press Ltd 1989

Translator's Foreword © Taeko Midorikawa 1989

First published in the United States of America in 1989

Printed in Hong Kong

ISBN 0–312–02444–4

Library of Congress Cataloging-in-Publication Data
Genbaku ni otto o ubawarete. English.
Widows of Hiroshima.
Translation of: Genbaku ni otto o ubawarete.
1. Hiroshima-shi (Japan)—History—Bombardment,
1945—Personal narratives. 2. Women—Japan—Hiroshima-
shi—Biography.   I. Kanda, Mikio, 1922—
II. Title.
D767.25.H6G46813   1989   940.54′25   88–18832
ISBN 0–312–02444–4

Contents

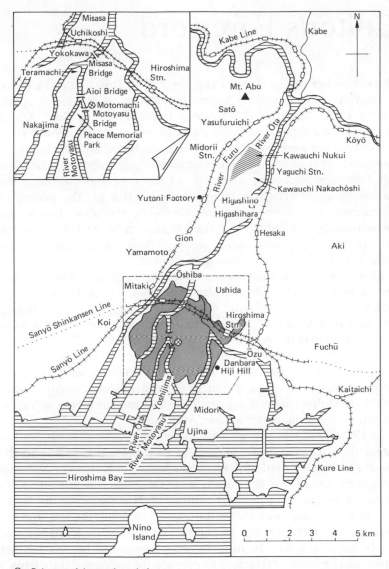

⊗ Epicentre of the atomic explosion

▨ Area completely destroyed by the atomic bomb

▤ Area where the Nukui widows live

Editor's Foreword

Hiroshima lies on the delta of the River Ōta. It is a city which was destroyed at 8.15 a.m. on 6 August 1945 by the atom bomb dropped from the US Airforce's B29 strategic bomber, 'Enola Gay'. Today Hiroshima is a thriving city with a population of just over 900 000.

Thirty-seven years have now passed since Hiroshima was bombed. People say that nowadays the devastation brought about by the atom bomb is remembered as a tragedy of the past and that even the harrowing experience is a fading memory. But for the people of Hiroshima, who have direct experience of the atom bomb, the memories are not fading, nor does the atom bomb belong to the distant past. They have never stopped their anti-war/anti-nuclear campaign, or their earnest appeals for peace.

This book is a record of my interviews with peasant wives who lost their husbands and children in the atom bombing, and of what they told me about their early life, marriage, suffering due to the bomb, and how they have lived since then. I conducted these interviews in Satō Township in the Asa Minami Ward of Hiroshima City (formerly Kawauchi Village in Asa District). Satō Township is an agricultural community in the suburbs of Hiroshima, which developed in the northern part of the delta, about 10 kilometres from the city centre. In this township, there is a place called Kawauchi Nukui, which is known as 'the atom-bomb widows' village'.

In 1945 Kawauchi was a small village of 550 households, with a population of about 2000. In June of that year, responding to the call for a decisive battle for the homeland, the Kawauchi National Volunteer Corps was organised, with the village headman, Kōta Masukawa (who died in the bombing of Hiroshima) at its head. Except for mothers with children under 3 years old, the sick and the wounded, all men between 16 and 60 and women up to 40 years of age became members. In July, an order was issued by Asa District Office of Hiroshima Prefecture to prepare for four days' duty from 3 August. The tasks assigned were to construct an airfield some 20 kilometres north-east of Kawauchi at Kamine in Neno Village, Takata District (present-day Yachiyo Township) and to dismantle buildings at Nakajima Shinmachi (the epicentre of the atomic explosion) in Hiroshima. Under the direction of the Ministry of Home Affairs, the work of dismantling buildings had been undertaken at 133 sites in Hiroshima, covering an area of 27 hectares. With regard to their assignment, representatives of the Nakachōshi Squad and Nukui Squad drew lots, and it was decided that the 191 members of the Nukui Squad were to go to Hiroshima.

At 8.15 a.m. on 6 August, the atom bomb exploded over the heads of the Nukui Squad, who had set about the work of dismantling buildings in high spirits. The entire city was thrown into a flaming hell and the Nukui Squad was completely annihilated. Only seven members of the squad returned to their village while all the others disappeared without trace. Even those seven were so severely burned that subsequently they all died.

As soon as the horrifying news was brought, the people of Nukui ran hither and thither among the ashes of Hiroshima searching for their loved ones. Yet even after a week or ten days had elapsed, virtually all remained missing; not a trace of them was to be found. Among those who could not give up hope of finding their loved ones were 75 wives who had lost their husbands. In Nukui Village misery reigned. In house after house, women had suddenly been widowed.

Thirty-seven years later, 26 of these widows are still to be found. All are very old women. The interviews in this book are with 19 of these women; those omitted were either invalids or had other problems. These 19 peasant wives overcame secondary radiation sickness, and their whole lives have been spent working in the fields trapped all along by the deep-rooted conventions of village society. They are a handful of living witnesses of the atom bombing.

This book is based on the articles entitled 'The Soil and the Passing Years – 36 Years in the Lives of Peasant Wives Widowed by the Atom Bomb', which were serialised in 53 issues of the Hiroshima edition of the *Nihon Nōgyō Shinbun* [*Japan Farming Newspaper*] between March and October 1981. Four more cases have been added to the biographies which appeared in the newspaper articles and all the material, in a revised form, is now appearing under one cover.

I should like to express my sincere gratitude to Mr Masao Fujiwara, Managing Director of the National News Information Office of the Federation of Agricultural Cooperative Associations, and Mr Masaru Arai, Chief Editor of *Nihon Nōgyō Shinbun*, for willingly giving permission to publish. I should also like to thank Mr Katsumi Sakamaki of the Editorial Division of Iwanami Shinsho for his kind endeavours in the editing and publishing of this book.

Last but not least, I should like to say thank you very much to everybody in the Nukui area for their cooperation. Grannies of Nukui! You are the living witnesses of the atom bomb. Please keep fit and live long!

Mikio Kanda, Editor
2 January 1982

Translator's Foreword

The total number of confirmed deaths arising from the atom bomb that was dropped on Hiroshima on 6 August 1945 is 148 177. The number for Nagasaki, where the atom bomb was dropped three days later, is 75 167. Taken together, these two bombs thus accounted for 233 344 deaths. However, it has been estimated that this huge figure is more than 100 000 less than the true number. In other words, it seems likely that two small-scale nuclear weapons killed about a third of a million people. Nor should we forget that the number of dead is still increasing. Even though it is now more than 40 years since the atom bombs were dropped, during the year August 1986 to August 1987 the total number of deaths arising from exposure to the atomic explosions were 4619 in Hiroshima and 2359 in Nagasaki. Hence the final curtain has still not come down on the tragedy of Hiroshima and Nagasaki.

After their husbands and their children were killed by the atom bomb from an American B29, the Nukui widows were plunged into a 'living hell'. Yet strange to say, when they talk about their experiences, one does not hear from them a single word of criticism of America. Some readers might think that, considering what these women went through, it would have been reasonable for them to feel anger towards America. But for my part, it is very impressive that the agony and the sadness which these women experienced has produced a response which has gone beyond the narrow confines of denouncing America and instead has reached the level of denouncing war. One never hears them saying: 'America was wrong. I hate America.' What one hears instead is: 'War was wrong. I hate war.' Like the majority of women in pre-war Japan, these Nukui widows were not highly educated people. And yet it seems to me that theirs is a wisdom which has allowed them to perceive the very heart of the matter.

There were many occasions as I was translating the stories of these Nukui widows when I felt so choked that I could not continue. But whenever it happened, I would pull myself together and carry on, thinking that their stories deserved to be heard by as wide an audience as possible. Since they spoke in broad Hiroshima dialect, translating their stories into English was no easy task. Often it was a time-consuming struggle to convert just one of their earthy turns of phrase

xiii

into an appropriate English expression. If the English version as it appears here reads at all naturally or colloquially, my thanks are due to John Crump for this. In fact, at least half of the work of this translation has been his. Without his cooperation this book would never have appeared.

Since the Japanese edition of this book was published in 1982, three of the Nukui widows whose stories appear here – Setsuko Nishimoto, Ochika Matsuda and Midori Matsumoto – have passed away.

Those without a specialist knowledge of Japan may find helpful some background information on a few of the terms which appear frequently in this book.

Dismantling Houses
This measure was enforced in order to create open spaces within Japanese cities, which would make fires started by air raids more easily controllable. The first such order, covering Tokyo and Nagoya, was issued by the Ministry of Home Affairs on 26 January 1944. All buildings in the designated areas were subject to compulsory dismantling. Subsequently, compulsory dismantling of buildings was undertaken in various other cities, including Hiroshima, and on occasions army tanks were used for this purpose. The government had no policy for compensating those whose houses or shops were dismantled, nor did it offer any assistance for their relocation.

Volunteer Corps
On 13 June 1945, the Imperial Rule Assistance Association and its affiliated bodies were dissolved in order to create the National Volunteer Combat Corps. Then, on 23 June, the Volunteer Corps Military Service Law was promulgated. Under its provisions, men between 15 and 60 and women between 17 and 40 had to enrol in the National Volunteer Combat Corps.

Delivery to the Authorities
Due to the shortage of labour and lack of fertiliser, the crop yields in 1945 decreased sharply to 65 per cent of pre-war levels. Despite this, delivery quotas were increased and in March 1947 the Occupation authorities and the Japanese government gave orders that the police were to enforce delivery of crops by the farmers. The result of this forced delivery was that the small farmers found that most of their crops were requisitioned and they were driven to the edge of

starvation. Needless to say, virtually all the families described in this book belonged to the category of small farmers.

A word about the method of counting ages is also required. The Nukui widows count ages according to the traditional method used throughout East Asia. According to this method, a person is already 1 at the time of birth, and that person's age increases by 1 at every subsequent New Year. Thus there is no straightforward method of rendering ages counted in this traditional fashion into Western-style ages.

In this book, the convention has been followed that comments by the editor are enclosed in round brackets, while comments by the translator are in square brackets.

Taeko Midorikawa, Translator
August 1987, York

1   Setsuko Nishimoto

1 We Were an Odd Couple, But . . .
Setsuko Nishimoto

Work, work . . .

These days I'm getting a bit doddery and I often forget things. I wonder if I can tell you what you want . . .

I was born on 10 April. I'm 80, you know. My eldest sister was called Setsume, the next was Kiyome, and my young brother was called Masabu. So I was the third girl. There were four of us kids.

My Dad was called Eikichi, but he died when I was 3, so I don't remember much about him. My Mum was called Otsuru, just like the Pilgrim Otsuru in the old story. She was widowed early, with four kids on her hands. It was ten months after my young brother Masabu was born, just about when he was starting to crawl. She was widowed young and brought up four kids, so my Mum had a really hard time of it. She died after the war, when she was 88. Together with her kids, she was a peasant, working 6 *tan* [about 1½ acres] of paddy fields.

We lived in a place called Higashino in Yasufuruichi, and when I came home from school (Higashino Elementary School) I used to help with the farmwork. I'd spread out unhulled rice to dry on as many as fifty or sixty straw mats. In those days, we went back home from school to eat our dinner and, during my dinner break, I'd turn by hand the unhulled rice to air it. Then I'd run back to school. Sometimes before going to school in the morning, I'd put on straw sandals and tread the barley, and then go to school. Together with my Mum, I worked really hard. I grew up really seeing how hard life is for a widowed peasant woman. I think it was thanks to my Mum that even after I was widowed by the atom bomb I could manage the farmwork.

My Mum was never ill once. She lived to be 88. After you've been widowed, you can't afford to be ill or anything like that. Sometimes I think it might be nice to put my feet up, but I've never been ill either. Even when I had my babies, I didn't stay in bed more than a few days.

1

It was no easy task doing the farmwork without a man about the place. My Mum and us kids held on to the 6 *tan* [1¹/₂ acres] of paddy fields. We all made our own straw sandals. We made them ourselves at night, and then put them on to go to school. My Mum didn't have a farthing to spare, even to buy us clogs. Ever since I was a kid, things haven't gone smoothly.

Us kids grew up knowing only hard work, then Masabu was killed by the atom bomb, and both my sisters died four or five years ago. Now it's only me who's left. It's ended up that no one on our old farm has got family ties with my Mum and Dad. My Mum and Dad's grave is there, but there doesn't seem much point in going there now.

I got married towards the end of 1919. My husband was called Tsunezō and he was nine years older than me. I think that he might have been getting on for 27. In those days, they didn't put you in the family register until you had a baby, so I don't remember the exact day. . . People used to say about this place: 'Don't send your daughter as a bride to Nukui or Nakachōshi; there's not much to eat there.' What sort of fate brought me here I don't know, but anyway this is where I came to get married. We never saw each other before we got married. It was decided by our parents. I didn't know what sort of man I was marrying.

My husband was a heavy drinker and a very hard man to live with. Even when I was suckling the baby, he would hurry me up and say 'Get back to work quickly!' But however much I tried to hurry the baby, babies don't drink that fast. I used to really get in a sweat. My husband used to love drinking with his mates. When they were really drinking, I reckon they would put away 7 or 8 *shō* [13 or 14 litres] of *saké* between them. He was the sort of man, whenever he met someone, he'd bring them home and tell them: 'Drink up; eat up!' He went to the local pubs a lot too.

Even when there was nothing in it for him, he still got a kick out of helping people. He was the kind of man who went out of his way to help people, even if they didn't ask him. So when he was killed by the atom bomb, the folks round here said 'Your old man was a nice person' and everybody missed him. But inside the house, he was a bit of a tyrant, you know.

It was generally only at New Year and the *Bon* Festival [in summer] that I got the chance to go back to my Mum's house. My husband never bought me even a single thing. I suppose there wasn't any money to buy things for me because it all went on drink. I shouldn't tell you this, but I lost count of the number of times I ran away back to my Mum's house.

The world's a funny old place and because my husband helped people a lot, after I was widowed, the folks round here helped me a lot. You never know your luck.

I had eight kids. The eldest boy was called Shigeto, and when he was 22 he went off as a soldier. He was killed in the war on 23 August 1943. He was in the Signals Corps. The second boy was Yoshiaki. At the time of the atom bomb he was in the Clothing Depot in Kure. The third boy, Akio, was working in the Mitsubishi Shipyard. The fourth boy, Morito, was in Manchuria with the Manchuria/Mongolia Reclamation Youth Volunteer Corps. He came back in 1947. The fifth boy was called Kazuyuki and he was 3 at the time of the atom bomb. The eldest girl was called Takae and she was in the second year of higher elementary school. When the pupils were mobilised, she was sent to the Clothing Depot in Yoshijima. Chieko, the second girl, was in the fifth year of elementary school; and Toyoko, the third girl, was 6.

I brought up eight kids, so it was nothing but work, work, work. To make ends meet, I didn't buy even a single *kimono* for myself. With so many kids, I had a really hard time of it. My whole life has been a penance.

I've never even put on any face-cream

I had one child after another, so with the baby strapped on my back, I'd rear any number of silkworms and do all the other jobs. By day, I'd work my heart out in the fields and at night I'd be busy grinding grain. The grinding place was at the entrance to the yard, and I'd light a lamp or a lantern and do the grinding there. You worked it by foot, so it was really hard work.

There weren't any paddy fields here, so we had to eat barley. And we made dumplings out of millet. Nowadays, I often talk about it with Old Mother Takasaki (Haru Takasaki) and we say to each other: 'Why was it that in the old days, all we had to eat was barley?' Around here, even the rich folk ate barley.

I used to work most nights. It was the same for every family. I'd do work like spinning hemp to make the thread for *tatami* matting. And I used to go to Hiroshima to collect nightsoil for fertiliser. I wouldn't get any sleep some nights, going to collect nightsoil. There was never a night that I went to bed without doing some work first.

Often I'd only get two or three hours' sleep. So whenever I sat down, sleep would soon catch up with me and I'd start to doze, and then my husband would tell me off.

I'd boil up rice and barley in a huge pot, but even if I left a whole potful, it would soon all be gone. That's what happens when you have so many kids.

Like I said before, I was a good manager; from getting married to being widowed, I didn't buy a single *kimono* for myself. I made my own working clothes and the kids' things, by cutting up the clothes I brought with me when I got married. I even made mattress covers out of my old clothes. Before I got married, I worked for a while as a spinner in a mill in Higashihara (in Gion), so I brought with me a chest of drawers full of cotton *kimonos*, and I made do with those.

It was just before the atom bomb that women started to wear *monpe* trousers. The Women's National Defence Association, or whatever it was called, gave us the order 'Wear *monpe* trousers!' So although I'd never done it before, I cut up a *kimono* and made some.

Before we had *monpe*, we just used to tuck up our *kimonos* when we worked. Underneath, we wore our slips short too. In summer we were really bitten by mosquitoes. I'd burn wood to heat the bath or do other jobs with the baby strapped to my back, and the mosquitoes would be biting the baby's legs. So I used to hitch up my *kimono* and cover the baby's legs. When I think about it now, it's hard to believe. I shouldn't think that young people these days would put up with even for one hour with what we used to do in those days.

I've said it before, but I had so many kids that I had a really hard time of it and life was a penance. My husband was a heavy drinker and he didn't give me any money. He didn't buy anything for me either. All he ever said was: 'Get on with your work, get on with your work!' Yet all *he* ever did was pass the time of day with the neighbours and pop in here and there to drink *saké*.

Other couples used to work together as man and wife, but our house was different. I wouldn't have minded the work if we had done it together as a couple, but working on my own really got on my nerves. I used to think: 'I can't put up with it any more.' It was because I was so fed up that I'd run away to my Mum's house. My husband or the neighbours would come to fetch me, and I'd end up going back. If it were nowadays, it would probably have come to divorce in the end, I suppose. We were an odd couple.

'I must put up with it for the kids' sake', I'd think to myself, and so I'd get on with my work. I worked harder than other people, or you might say I did two people's work. Around here (in Nukui) it was only me who had so many kids and such a hard time of it, so I had to strain every nerve, just like a man might. When I got married, I brought some face-cream with me and I've still got it, you know. I was busy and always working, so I never got round to putting on any cream. I've never once used powder or cream. I've never had the time for such things.

You might not believe it, but people say that if you use a lot of powder when you're young, you'll get wrinkles on your face when you're old. I never used any make-up, so that must be why I don't have any wrinkles, mustn't it? I bet I've got the best complexion out of all the people you've interviewed. Aren't I right? . . . The folks round here all say: 'You wouldn't think Old Mother Nishimoto was 80; she's got such a good complexion.' Don't you think so too?

Searching for his gold teeth

On the morning of the 6th (6 August 1945), my husband said: 'I don't much feel like going today; I don't want to go.' He felt what was coming, I suppose. It's true; if he hadn't gone, he'd have been saved from the atom bomb . . . But since all the other folks round here were going . . .

My husband walked away holding the reins of the horse and cart. Four or five neighbours were on the cart, and they were hoping to bring back some wood from the dismantled buildings and share it out between them.

When it happened, I was in the lav. I thought it was just like a flash of lightning; and next there was a noise like an enormous BANG. Inside the house, it went pitch dark. The sliding doors and *shōji* screens tumbled down and, perhaps because there was nowhere else for the wind to go, that wall over there fell right out. When I looked over towards Hiroshima, a black cloud rose up. I thought to myself that a bomb had fallen. Over towards Mitaki, it had burst into flames. I was thinking that my husband would be helping with the clearing up after the bomb.

About 3 o'clock, the loudspeaker said: 'Hiroshima is completely destroyed.' I was surprised because I'd been thinking that my husband was doing things like clearing up after the bomb. Even so, I never thought that he'd be dead, but I couldn't settle, thinking to myself: 'I wonder what he's doing?' Even when evening came, my husband didn't come back. I couldn't go to sleep. I heard later that the atom bomb went off during his roll-call on Aioi Bridge (the epicentre of the atomic explosion).

In the middle of the night of the 6th, I heard that the survivors had come back to Yutani (Yutani Heavy Industry Factory in Gion – refuge centre for those injured by the bomb), so straightaway I set off. A big crowd of people were saying: 'Give me some water!' 'Let me drink some water!' They were all charred and it was horrible to watch.

At the entrance place, Old Man Nomura (Kiyoto Nomura) had a wound on his head and was covered with blisters. When he saw me, he said: 'Hasn't my family come . . . ?'

'Well, I didn't see them . . .'

'Oh! Your husband said he was going back. On the way, we got separated. Hasn't he got back yet?'

Old Man Nomura still had his strength. He said: 'Your husband won't be among these people.' When I heard that, I quickly turned back home, but my husband hadn't got back. So, thinking that he might have collapsed on the way, immediately I went out again, but the road was dark and I couldn't make out anything. I let Mrs Nomura know and, doing one thing and another, daybreak came. I heard later that Mrs Nomura set off straightaway, but her husband was already dead . . .

On the morning of the 7th, I took Akio with me and we set off for Hiroshima to look for my husband. We walked along peering at the dead bodies, covered with blisters, on the roadside and the river bank. We peered into the air-raid shelters too. They were full of dead bodies piled up. They were all charred, you know . . .

Because they were all charred, I couldn't tell which was my husband. Then I had an idea. He had a lot of gold teeth, so I thought that if I could find them, I'd know.

After that, I walked on and whenever I came across someone who looked like my husband, I would open the mouth of the charred body and look for gold teeth. I wonder how many dozens, or even hundreds, of dead mouths I opened and looked in. I was desperate, so I didn't even think that it was scary. I just did it, thinking to myself, 'Isn't this him?' as I searched for his gold teeth.

For two more days, on the 8th and the 9th of August, I went out looking for him. By the 8th, the dead bodies were already covered in maggots and flies, and the smell was awful. It was a really peculiar smell, you know. There were dead bodies everywhere. I even peered into the mouths of the slimy dead bodies that had been pulled out of the river. So I walked on, peering into mouths, looking for his gold teeth. As time went by, you couldn't tell whether they were gold teeth or maggots. It was terrible. . . For three days we walked all over, looking for him, but in the end my husband wasn't found. I had trouble sleeping because, for a time, whenever I closed my eyes I could still see those poor dead bodies. I'd sometimes think to myself: 'Why did so many people come to such a terrible end? They all went off because they were told that it was for the good of the country . . .'

We waited and waited, but my husband didn't come back. The horse never came back either. I couldn't settle down even to my work. I was at a loss what to do and my head was empty. It was as though I'd lost my wits.

About one week later, a fever came on and I had a temperature as high as 40°C [105°F]. If I so much as smoothed down my hair, it dropped out. Akio was the same. Both of us were laid up (with radiation sickness). We boiled up the *dokudami* herb and drank it as medicine. People said that the hair of the *manmankibi* plant was good for you, so we boiled that up too and drank it as medicine. But my temperature wouldn't go down, and my hair kept on falling out. It got really thin.

After four or five days, my temperature went down. Still my husband hadn't come back. 'If he's dead, somehow we ought to bury him', I thought to myself. I'd got his tobacco pouch and his pipe, so I burnt the tobacco pouch down by the river and collected the ashes. Together with the ashes, we buried his pipe, without burning it, in the grave. I thought to myself 'That's his soul', and I pray at his grave even now.

Akio gets his call-up papers on 12 August

On 12 August, Akio got his call-up papers. He was ordered to enlist in the Second Corps of the Hiroshima Division on the 15th . . . Akio had got a high temperature after going out to look for his Dad, and his hair had fallen out, so when his call-up papers came, he was still shaky on his feet.

Early on the morning of the 15th, I packed up some food and set off to Hiroshima with Akio. Dead bodies were still lying around everywhere!

The Second Corps' barracks had been burnt down, and after his business was finished, Akio came out. He said:

'I've just eaten the rice gruel that they gave us in a length of bamboo. Hiroshima is completely destroyed, so the Second Corps is going to Yamaguchi. We'll get on the train about mid-day tomorrow.' When I heard this, I went back home. That night, Akio slept rough at Hiroshima Station with the other conscripts.

Early on the morning of the 16th, I packed some food and hurried to Hiroshima Station. Mid-day was drawing close, and it was when Akio was about to get on the express that a voice said: 'Discharged from military service'. I felt like I'd been bewitched. The two of us made our way home, walking along under the hot, mid-day sun without saying a word. When I think about it now, it was really odd. I suppose that even after Hiroshima had been completely destroyed, they were calling up soldiers and the military still wanted to fight on. When I think about it now, it was a completely daft thing to do.

When I became a widow, I was 44. We had about 5 *tan* [1¼ acres]. The children were small, so I worked on my own. In 1947, Morito – my fourth boy – came back from Manchuria. He worked on the farm and that made things a bit easier for me, but still there was so much work to do that at nights I went short of sleep. Even when I was sick, I couldn't afford to stay in bed.

I'd get up at 2 o'clock in the morning, load a couple of tubs on my handcart, and set off to collect nightsoil. The handcart had iron-rimmed wheels and the lane was stony, so it was really heavy. On the way there, I'd load up vegetables and take them as far as Tōkaichi. To get the nightsoil, I had to go as far as places like Ujina and Danbara. If I didn't take them vegetables or something, they wouldn't give me any nightsoil. What I had to take was a little grain or some vegetables. Two or three times, I was caught by the police. Once they even came and searched inside the house. When they saw our tubs and bins, they thumped them. They even went upstairs, and rummaged about in the straw.

I only had a woman's strength, so I could only manage to bring back a couple of tubs. I'd go to collect nightsoil seven or eight times a month, and I'd often get one of the kids to push the cart with me as I pulled. I'd wake up one of the kids who was going to elementary school and say: 'I'm sorry. I know you're sleepy, but could you help push the cart?' Even now, the kids still talk about it. They say: 'I can still hear Mum's voice saying, "Could you help push the cart?"'

When the girls got into about the fourth year of elementary school, one after another they did the cooking for me. All my time went on things like going to get nightsoil and working in the fields. Anyway, I was working my heart out just to support the kids.

I used to thin the nightsoil with water. If you don't use nightsoil, the crops don't grow. I had to hand over all my painfully grown crops to the government. The kids got only half a cup of rice each as their ration. It wasn't enough for growing children. I used to feed them by spinning out their rice with sweet potatoes and *mouli* . . . Anyway, somehow I managed to feed them. As long as you feed them, they grow. Because we were farming, there was food to eat and I could bring them up somehow. If we hadn't been farming, I reckon we would have ended up killing ourselves.

We were short of firewood too. I used to go to Nukui Hill (a wood owned in common by the village) to gather two loads of firewood in the morning and two loads in the afternoon. I used to go to gather up the fallen pine needles too. We got a ration of firewood, but it wasn't much. We couldn't afford to buy any, so it was work, work all the time. What with all this, I wore myself out. I've got aches in my hips and shoulders and bones. Now I'm just a bundle of aches.

School books, too, weren't free like they are now. I let my three daughters go to high school. If I didn't let them go to high school, I thought they wouldn't be able to make a good marriage. They all made the effort to work their way through school and did very well.

On 6 August, I always go to pray at the Seigan Temple and at the monument to the Volunteer Corps (in the Peace Memorial Park in Hiroshima). They often say to me, 'Since we've come this far, let's go to the cinema or the shops', but I've never gone even once. If I'd spent money on myself, I couldn't have managed to get my daughters married. If I hadn't saved every penny, I couldn't have afforded to get them married. When my daughters got married, I let them take everything they needed – even tea for the pot. Even these days, there aren't many parents who do that much. I did everything for them.

I say to my children: 'Don't come running to your Mum. You've got to grin and bear it, and stand on your own two feet.' And I say to them: 'For the sake of your kids, get on well together as man and wife, and live long lives.' It's no fun being a widow.

Youngsters today seem to think that if war broke out, it would be exciting. There's nothing exciting about it. It's just stupid. Youngsters forget that war means dying. They don't know how cruel war is. Youngsters walk along the embankment at the back of our house, singing war songs. They don't know what war means. They didn't live through the hard times of the war, so it seems to them that war is exciting and something flashy. I tell my children and my grandchildren just what it was like during the war. War mustn't happen again.

These days, ships are coming with nuclear weapons on board, and they're building warships. If they keep on building up the Self Defence Forces, there's bound to be another war. When armaments keep on piling up year by year, it must come to a full-scale war in the end. If another war comes, Japan will be completely destroyed. There mustn't be another war.

Morning and evening, I chant a sutra. Thanks to the spirits of the dead, we are living on. You need more than your own strength to keep on living. In our house, people go off to work early in the morning, so my daughter-in-law boils up the rice in the evening. That's why we offer hot rice to the spirits of the dead in the evening. We freshened up the household altar to the Buddha. We thought the dead would be pleased.

Even when you're getting on in years, it doesn't do just to take it easy. I read the newspaper with a magnifying glass. I keep on using my brains. I talk to the youngsters about the things I read in the newspaper.

Today the others are boxing up cucumbers. My job is the weeding. During the day, there's no one about the house. Everybody's hard at work, growing the crops. If you're going to telephone, better make it of an evening. Then I'll be in . . .

2   Tsuruyo Monzen

2 All the Tortures of This World Made into One

Tsuruyo Monzen

Hard work in the fields

I've got a bad leg, so please excuse my bad manners, sitting this way.

I was born on 20 April 1905 into a farming family in a place called Kita Shimoyasu, in Gion, in Asa District. I was the eldest girl and next came the eldest boy, Kakuji, who died young, when he was 25. When he was examined for conscription, they found that he'd got a bad chest. After Kakuji, there was my younger sister, Natsumi. There were three of us kids.

When I was a young girl I used to spend my time, from morning till night, weaving *tatami* matting. We used to grow a lot of rushes. We planted them when winter came and harvested them in the heat of August. Then we'd use them for making *tatami*. When I came home from school (Gion Elementary School), I wasn't told 'Get on with your homework!'; it was always 'Spin the hemp!' I used to soak the dried hemp in water the day before and, when I came home from school, I'd work the hemp with something a bit like a comb.

When we got into the fifth or sixth year of elementary school, we didn't play any more. As soon as we got back home, we were told 'Spin the hemp!' or 'Make the warp!' So you can see, children too worked really hard. The warp used to make a twanging sort of noise and we wound it into balls around one of those 'spool' sort of things. Children all helped with the jobs that had to be done first before you could weave the *tatami*.

The way I'm talking about it might be all mixed up, but you write it down nicely for me . . .

I hated the smell of rushes. I thought it would be a good idea to go some place where there wouldn't be that smell, so I came here to get married. I was 18 at the time. It was May 1922. It was about the time of the year when lots of fireflies were on the wing. I didn't want to get married at all. Even on the evening before my marriage, I said I was going to collect fireflies and, just as I was about to go out, my mother really told me off. When it comes to the point of getting married, everybody is in two minds about it. But, being a man, perhaps you don't understand that sort of thing.

In the old days, once you'd passed 20, they called you 'a 20-year-old granny'. I had the feeling that my mother wanted to marry me off early because she was my father's second wife. I suppose she was scared that people might say that because she was a second wife, she wanted to use her daughter about the house and wouldn't let her marry early. So the way it turned out, she tried to marry me off young.

My relatives made the arrangements and I got married. I came to a place where they didn't grow rushes and left behind my village where the fireflies flew around.

My husband was called Giichi and he was nine years older than me. When the atom bomb was dropped, he was 50. He was a really good man and we never even had a single row. Oh, wait a minute! Perhaps we did have one row about our boy who was killed in the war. That's right; we certainly did have just that one row. I nearly told you a lie . . .

My husband was on the big side and he kept the best of health. After getting married, my first baby was born the next year and after that I had seven more. You might say the babies just kept on coming. Well, in the old days everybody had big families.

My husband had only brothers and there were four of them altogether. My husband was the oldest. The next, Denichi, was killed in the war. The third, Tomeichi, fell ill and died in 1944. The fourth, Teruichi, was killed in the war when his ship was sunk in the South Seas. So my husband's brothers were all either killed in the war or died from illness.

We had 8 *tan* [about 2 acres] of land. About 4 *tan* [1 acre] of that was rented. We only had dry fields and no paddy fields, so it was really hard work. In the morning, we got up when it was still dark, and at night we worked in the fields till the siren sounded at 9 o'clock. My mother-in-law used to say to me 'Come back home a little bit earlier', but if I'd gone back earlier like she said, the work wouldn't have been done. For one thing, we had to turn over the soil by hand with our hoes. And for another, we grew a lot of crops like millet. While it was light, we did things like thinning out the crops and, when night came on and it got so that you couldn't see anything, we'd do things like stripping the husk from the millet and digging up the soil. It was such hard work, I'll never forget it.

Collecting firewood was women's work

Mouli and burdock grew well in Kami Nukui. In winter we grew
mainly barley and in summer we grew millet and perhaps 3 *tan* [³/₄
acre] of barley. About three years after I got married, we started to
grow indigo plants which they used for dying cloth. We used to dry
masses of them on the stony riverside of the River Furu. We'd make
them into bundles and then the dealer would buy them and take
them away. We grew them for about four or five years, I suppose.
On the other hand, we grew hemp for quite a long while.

For collecting nightsoil, we used an ox-cart and then, later on, we
changed to a horse. My husband would load up six to eight tubs. For
a time after we got married, he used the boat to go up and down the
River Furu. The boat didn't rock very much so he could load up a
lot of tubs. We had a big cesspit on the edge of the field and we'd
carry the tubs there on a pole over our shoulders. There were some
boundary-trees by the field, and I'm not so tall, as you can see, so I
was always bumping into them and spilling the nightsoil. My husband
liked everything to be just so, so he made me wash clean the tubs.
On cold days, it was really awful work. Looking back on it now, it's
hard to believe what I used to do. In the end, my body had to pay
for it and now I've got aches all over.

On the far side of Mount Abu (586 metres), there was Nukui Hill.
I remember too that I used to go all the way there and back to collect
firewood. Firewood was always in short supply round here. Going to
the hills to collect firewood was women's work:

> To collect nightsoil, the men to Hiroshima go;
> To collect firewood, the women to the hills go . . .

But you could hardly make a song out of it, could you!

Even on cold days, I'd have climbed to the Pass of Mount Abu by
6 o'clock in the morning. To get there was uphill all the way and
beyond the Pass was really hard going. Just to get to Nukui Hill took
more than one hour, and I'd go there with four or five of the
neighbours. It was really hard work, but you had the others for
company, so that kept you going. It was the custom on Nukui Hill
that the early-comers had the pick of the firewood. We had to collect
enough firewood to see us through the winter, so it was a really big
job. We used to stock up a pile of it, under the eaves, round the
back of the house.

If it was one load, I'd leave home early in the morning and get back about 4 o'clock. If it was two loads, it was a whole day's work. Now and again, I'd do what we called 'sending two loads'. Getting to the hill, I'd cut enough firewood for two loads. Then I'd carry one load and set it down some way along the path. Then I'd go back and carry the other load as far as the one I'd left. Doing this over and over again, I'd end up bringing back two loads in one day. I'd come back with the firewood neatly bundled in the wooden frame on my back.

Around here, they used to say 'wood first, rice second'. People said that to go without wood was harder to bear than to go without rice. My mother-in-law often used to thank me when I came back from the hill with firewood on my back. She'd say:

'You have made a big pile. It looks like a mountain of treasure. As long as we've got as much firewood as this, it'll be all right, whatever happens.'

My mother-in-law knew what hard work it was because she too had been bringing back firewood ever since her young days. I suppose that's why she used to thank me like that.

In the kitchen, you had to make sure that the water jar was always full of water; otherwise people said that you were no good as a daughter-in-law. In the old days, we all had wells. Outside in the garden, there'd be the well. We'd draw up water in a bamboo bucket and pour it into a wooden pail. Then we'd take it to fill up the bath or the water jar. It was really hard, carrying water to the bath or to the kitchen. It used to wear me out!

Later, we fixed up a pulley for the bucket and that made it a lot easier. I had one baby after another and I had to draw up the water even when my tummy was big. It did you no good at all, bringing in water from the outside well not long after you'd had a baby. We used to heat the bath with firewood.

My mother-in-law passed away in August 1937. She always used to thank me for working like a beaver. Oh, I'm going over the same ground again, aren't I?

The empty box of ashes

I brought up as many as eight kids, you know. Nowadays people don't have so many children, but before the war they used to tell us: 'Produce children; increase the population.' So we had children, even though we knew it made life hard.

Let's see if I can tell you about the way things were around the time when the atom bomb was dropped. Our eldest boy, Toshio, went off to fight in the hot countries with the Southern Expeditionary Force. He was a lucky lad. Before the end of the war, we got an official letter to say that he'd been killed. We'd given him up, thinking he was not coming back and then he suddenly turned up after the war had ended. I can't tell you how happy I was to see him turn up alive. In 1980, he passed away before me, from high blood pressure. He was 55.

The next boy was Tadao. The official letter, saying that he'd been killed in the South Sea Islands, was delivered from the village office on a cold February day after the war had ended in 1946. When I looked at it, it said that he'd 'been killed in the South Sea Islands on 27 July 1944'. He volunteered for the Fleet Air Arm and so he left Matsumoto Commercial School (in Hiroshima) ahead of time. We told him: 'You could still join the Navy after finishing school first.'

But he went off, saying: 'If we don't go now, Japan won't win.'

He was 17 and it was a really brave thing to do. He really believed that it was for the good of the country . . . Just once we got a military postcard from him, saying: 'I'm in Taiwan.'

When the war ended, I expected Tadao to come back too, but he didn't come. I didn't know that he'd been killed in 1944. It was a good six months after the war had ended that I got the official letter, saying that he'd been killed. It was really heartbreaking. I thought that he'd ended up throwing his young life away for nothing.

Talking of Tadao, let me tell you something else to do with him. It was soon after I got the official letter, saying that he'd been killed, in February 1946. A letter came, telling me to come and collect Tadao's ashes. I felt really grateful, so I smartened myself up and went to Kaita Temple (in Kaitaichi, Aki District) to collect Tadao's remains.

They had the remains of about ten people there. When the priest had finished chanting the sutra, an official – I don't know which official he was – gave me Tadao's remains. Carefully, I let him hang the box, with Tadao's ashes in it, round my neck. Thinking to myself, 'Tadao's in here', I hugged the box. But do you know, that box was really light and somehow I felt it wasn't right. All the same, I thought to myself that something of Tadao's, or perhaps his (Buddhist) name tablet, was inside. So I said thank you very much to the people for their help and left the temple. I got on a train at Kaitaichi Station. With the box round my neck, I went as far as Yokokawa Station, hugging it tightly all the way. There, the official, who had come that far with me, gave me a piece of paper and said: 'It is written here that a lump sum is due to your son Tadao, who died in the war.'

While I was waiting at Yokokawa Station for the Kabe line train, I started to think to myself: 'This lump sum belongs to Tadao, so let's put it into the box.' I undid the white cloth, took off the lid, and looked inside. What do you think was there? There was nothing at all inside the box! Do you know, it was just empty!

The box gave off a nasty smell of pine resin. You know, I'd been hugging that box all the way to Yokokawa Station, thinking to myself that Tadao's ashes couldn't be inside because it was so light. But all the same, I'd been hugging it tightly because I thought that, in place of Tadao's ashes, at least there'd be his name tablet or a slip of paper with his name written on it. It was really heartbreaking to find it empty. I've never been treated so badly as that in all my life. I really felt as though I was going mad.

I didn't feel like pressing on to Midorii Station (on the Kabe line) with that box hanging round my neck any more. There I was, sitting all alone on a bench on Yokokawa Station, clutching that box with its nasty smell of pine resin and crying to myself. I felt so sad for Tadao, remembering the way he'd said: 'If we don't go now, Japan won't win.' Anyway, I pulled myself together, put into the box the piece of paper about the lump sum due to Tadao, and said to him: 'Let's go home, Tadao!' So I went back home from Yokokawa Station, hugging the empty box and crying all the way.

You might say that that sort of thing happened all the time just after the war but, all the same, what those officials did to us was still a terrible thing to do. I didn't put the official letter or the slip of paper about the lump sum due to Tadao into the household altar to the Buddha. Tadao didn't come back in the box that those officials gave us. He only lives in my memory.

The house was a right old mess

I'd better get on and say a word about the other kids. I've just told you about the eldest boy, Toshio, and the next boy, Tadao. Next I'll say something about our girl, Sachiko.

About the time that the atom bomb fell, she was in the second year of Gion Secondary Girls' School. When the pupils were mobilised, she went to work in the Post Office in front of Hiroshima Station. She came back soon after the atom bomb fell, with one half of her body burnt. It would have been about 10 o'clock, and she had on only one of her clogs . . . One side of her vest and one side of her *monpe* trousers had gone, and what was left of them was in tatters. I suppose the flash from the atom bomb got her on just one side of her body. Her back was covered with blood. She said that her friend's blood must have got on to her as they ran away, helping each other along. But she wasn't injured and so she didn't die. Mind you, all her hair fell out afterwards and she was completely bald. But nowadays, she's married and living in Yamamoto in Gion, and she's well now.

Our third boy, Tadashi, didn't live long, so he was already dead when they dropped the atom bomb. Our fourth boy, Masayoshi, was in the first year of higher elementary school. The fifth boy, Masao, was in the sixth year of elementary school. The sixth boy, Hiroshi, was in the first year of elementary school. The seventh boy was called Shizuyuki, and he was 4. So now I've told you about all my kids, eight altogether.

My husband was in the Volunteer Corps and they were sent to work on the 4th, 5th and 6th of August. On the morning of the 6th, we got up early. Like I said before, round here we were short of firewood, so he'd been bringing back wood from the buildings they'd been dismantling.

It had been decided by lot that my husband would take the horse and cart on the 6th. About midnight, the air-raid warning sounded. We lowered the light and, as he got ready for going, he said:

'It'll be a good idea to load up with some of the dismantled wood, but they tell me that the horse won't budge if it gets hot. So I'd better set off as early as I can.'

He was waiting for the all-clear signal to sound. About 1 o'clock in the morning, the all-clear sounded, and as he set off, his parting words were:

'Today's the last day, so I'll load up and come back early before it gets hot.'

It was nice weather on the 6th. You know, after all these years, I can tell you that I got the order as well to turn out with the Volunteer Corps. My boy was 4 years old, so I asked the person in the neighbourhood association and he let me off. But he warned me:

'Everybody is turning out with the Volunteer Corps, so keep in your house most of the time, and don't do anything very noticeable.'

If I'd gone off as well on that morning, we'd both have been killed and the kids would have been left all on their own. It was a good thing that even one of us was left alive. If Shizuyuki hadn't been 4 at that time, I'd have been killed too.

Shizuyuki went off to catch tiddlers in the River Furu and I was in the back field, thinning out the millet. Even though the person had said 'Don't go out of the house', the millet was already as tall as me, so I couldn't leave the thinning out any longer. My husband had been rushed off his feet, what with building the airfield at Neno and village business, so we were well behind with the farmwork.

It happened when I was really putting my back into thinning out the millet. There was a blinding flash and I thought the sun had fallen out of the sky. I thought to myself that something terrible was happening, so I ran across the next field and threw myself into the bamboo wood. It used to be all bamboo trees around where Jōnan Middle School is now.

When I looked over towards Hiroshima from the bamboo wood, a great mass of smoke rose up, tottering from side to side. Something white almost seemed to come floating over in this direction. I was completely dazed, and then Shizuyuki shouted from the embankment in a big voice: 'Mummy, come quickly! The house is falling down!'

I suppose Shizuyuki had forgotten all about his tiddlers and had come dashing back. But even though he was shouting, I didn't come out of the wood straightaway, but called to him: 'You might get hurt, so hide yourself.'

Inside, the house was a right old mess. The ceiling had been pushed up more than 15 centimetres and the windows were all broken. You know, we got that ceiling mended only a little while ago.

If he hadn't called out to me, I wouldn't have known it was my husband

Sachiko told me when she came back that Hiroshima was a sea of fire. She had run away towards the east (east relative to the epicentre) and that was why she got back to us. In the yard, she said to me: 'I don't think Dad will come back . . .' I was beside myself, thinking: 'If she's right, what'll become of us?'

It was just after noon when the priest (of the Jyōgyō Temple) came to tell us:

'Mr Monzen has come back, so please go to him.'

I put a mattress on the cart and set off with Masayoshi and Tsuneto Kaneichi from next door. Tsuneto had injured his finger and that was why he hadn't gone off with the Volunteer Corps. It was a big help, his coming to lend a hand.

There were already lots of people, covered with burns, coming

along the road, running away from Hiroshima. There were people
going to collect their loved ones, and injured people making their
way home, all streaming past each other in a hurry and, in the midst
of it all, we made haste to Hiroshima, pulling our cart.

We were just coming up to Yokokawa Bridge when a voice said:
'Oh! You've come!'

I said: 'Is it you, Dad?'

When I looked closely, there was no mistaking Dad, and he said:
'Thanks very much for coming.'

I suppose the clothes he'd been wearing had all been burnt. He'd
just got on his vest and pants, and all that was left of his vest was the
bit around the neck and the front. He'd still got a puttee on his left
leg, but there was nothing on his right leg. His face had swollen up
and you couldn't make out where his eyes were. His hands were all
swollen too. His skin looked like it was cellophane and was hanging
off. Underneath, it looked all festered. He'd got on just one torn
chikatabi plimsoll on his left foot and he was supporting himself on
some sort of stick.

My husband called out to me and that was why I knew it was him.
He looked so terrible that if he hadn't called out I would never have
known it was him. All the same, I was lucky because there were
many people that day who set off with their carts to collect their
loved ones, but never found them.

My husband told us: 'It happened at Teramachi. A tile from the
temple roof hit me on the head and knocked me out.'

He had loaded up the timber from the dismantled buildings and
was on his way home with Jitsugo Furumoto, Gunichi Kamioke and
Old Man Nakaoka. He said: 'Yokokawa Bridge was on fire, so I
couldn't get across. I ended up wading across the river.'

Even though he'd got those terrible burns and injuries, I suppose
he'd really wanted to get back home as quickly as he could and had
struggled in our direction.

After we'd put him on the cart, my husband was quiet and didn't
say a word. I suppose he just felt relieved. We came back as far as
Yasu Shrine in Gion, where there was a first-aid post. There they
cut off the skin that was hanging from his hands and put on some oil
for him. My husband was quiet while they treated him. All he said,
so that it was just me who could hear him, was:

'I'd like to get home quickly and lie down on the *tatami* matting.'

He was really suffering, I suppose.

By the time we got back home, it was 6 o'clock in the evening.

After I helped him on to the mattress, he kept on saying, rubbing his leg all the while:

'Thanks very much for coming. It was good to see you . . .'

He was worried about what had happened to Mr Furumoto and Mr Kamioke, who'd been with him.

When night came, he kept trying to twist his hands round as he lay on the mattress. He was saying things like:

'Until we can see how the war's going, don't go into Hiroshima' and 'Go to Natsumi's (his younger brother) place tomorrow and see if you can help them.'

I hung up the mosquito net and while I was seeing to him, he looked at his burnt hands, which were all sore, and said:

'These hands should be all right in a couple of days.'

How could I say whether they would be all right or not? I'll always remember what a dreadfully quiet night it was.

He'd say, in a loud voice, 'Giddy up there!'

After my husband got back on the 6th, he kept on saying: 'Give me some water; give me some water.' The neighbours said: 'If you give him water, he'll soon die. Don't give him any water.' So I made him go without. On the 7th too, he kept on at me all the time: 'Give me some water; please give me some water from the kettle.' I didn't bring the kettle, but again and again I'd bring a little water in a glass and help him to sip through his swollen lips.

All the time, he'd got pus oozing out from his back and from his hands. He couldn't lie on his side or on his back, so he was lying face down. He just kept on saying: 'Give me some water; give me some water.' Pus dripped from his arms when he moved them, and it smelt really awful.

On the evening of the 8th, my husband started to get funny. He started saying: 'The strings of the mosquito net; the strings of the mosquito net . . .' Thinking to myself that it was hopeless, I said 'Dad! Here's some water!' and poured a little water into his mouth. But by now he'd stopped saying: 'Give me some water.' Even when I said 'The mosquito net's hung up properly', he just kept on: 'The strings of the mosquito net . . .'

Sachiko and me did everything we could to look after him. When night came on, the rotting smell of his burnt skin and pus inside the mosquito net was almost too much to bear. It was a terrible smell and so, again and again, I'd say 'You go out, Sachiko' and send her outside. His breath smelt terrible too. But I never left him; I stayed looking after him.

On the morning of the 9th, he started to gee-up the horse. He'd gee-up the horse, saying 'Giddy up there!', loudly clicking his tongue. I suppose he was imagining that he was making the horse and cart go quicker, thinking to himself that he wanted to get home soon. By now he'd stopped saying 'Give me some water'; now it was just 'Giddy up there!' His voice got frantically loud, as though he was squeezing it out from his throat. Day and night, without any rest, he just kept on and on geeing-up the horse. I suppose he wanted to get back home quickly with the horse.

After he started to gee-up the horse, he didn't take any more food or drink. I suppose his head had got funny. From the time when he started to say 'The strings of the mosquito net . . .,' I'd realised that it was all hopeless, but still it was almost too much to bear, to stay at the side of my husband as he kept on geeing-up the horse all the time and clicking his tongue. It broke my heart.

After he started to gee-up the horse, he didn't seem to understand what I was saying to him any more. In his own head, he didn't seem to know at all what he was saying, but still he kept on and on in a loud voice with his 'Giddy up there!' . . . As we watched over him, Sachiko and me said to each other: 'It's all up with Dad.' While he had been saying 'The strings of the mosquito net . . .,' he'd still had some wits left, but I suppose that by the time he started to gee-up the horse, he'd lost his wits. Meanwhile, he'd lifted his hand and started to search for something. He lifted his hand that was dripping with pus and searched for something in the air. I'd heard that when somebody starts to search for something, they're going to die. Thinking to myself: 'So the end's come at last. It'll be a release for Dad', I dabbed his swollen lips with water. Even so, he kept on geeing-up that horse. But as the night of the 9th wore on, his voice got weaker.

At 8 o'clock on the morning of the 10th, my husband breathed his last. He'd been in agony since the 6th, and even after he died the peaceful look of someone who's been released from agony never came back to his burnt and swollen face.

I heard that the others who came back and died said before dying, 'Look after the kids', but my husband didn't say a word about the kids. He just said 'Give me some water', and kept on geeing-up the horse, with his 'Giddy up there!' He died in agony. Even now the voice of my husband saying 'Giddy up there!' still rings in my ears clearly, and sometimes I can hear it just the way it sounded then.

I went down by the river and cried

The way my husband died was like all the tortures of this world made into one. There wasn't a chance to have a funeral or anything like that. It was such a disaster that it was as though the whole village had died. No one could manage to come. On the riverside beyond the embankment, groups of people were cremating their loved ones. We put my husband's body on the cart and, together with my kids, I took it to the riverside. We dug a hole in the sand, covered his body with firewood and cremated him.

Jitsugo Furumoto, who'd been on the way back with my husband after they'd loaded up the horse and cart with timber, died too on the morning of the 10th. Gunichi Kamioke died as well, within an hour of my husband's death. As for Old Man Nakaoka, he lived on for twenty days or so, but then died in the end.

We picked up my husband's bones and put them for a while in the household altar. I think we left them there until the village funeral service (9 September 1945). For a while, I just didn't feel like doing any farmwork. For two or three months, I couldn't pull myself together.

The riverside where we'd cremated my husband was a wide, open space and nobody came there of an evening. Toshio still hadn't come back from the war. It was when dusk came on that I used to feel saddest of all. I'd go down to the riverside and cry my heart out until it grew dark. I used to cry until I couldn't cry any more.

There were dozens of times that I had a good cry, and I think that helped me to start feeling like work again. When I went back home after a cry, the kids would ask me: 'What's the matter, Mum?' Before I knew it, more than being sad about my husband's death, I had started to worry about how to bring up our kids. So from then on, I threw myself into my work and did all I could.

Round about March 1946, my left leg started to give me pain because I'd been on my feet too much. I thought to myself that it might get better if I got it massaged and I made several visits to the massager at Midorii, but it swelled up and got so that I couldn't move it.

I made several visits as well to the 'Way of the People' faith-healer at Kabe and each time I put 10 *sen* into the collection. I thought to myself that if I stuck at it, it would cure me, but it was really hard putting in 10 *sen* every time I went. I couldn't keep on putting into the collection, so every night, after the kids were asleep, I'd go out on to the veranda and, facing towards Kabe, I'd say in my prayers:

'I'm sorry to have to pray from here, but please make me better.'

But there was no answer to my prayers and my leg didn't get better. It didn't help either being on my feet all the time working. In the end, I went to the hospital in Kabe. The doctor was surprised when he saw my leg, and said:

'How have you managed to put up with it all this time?'

I'd been thinking that I'd cure myself without spending a penny more than I had to, but it turned out to be a mistake. My left leg had periostitis and the right one had arthritis, so they drew off some fluid for me. I was back and forth to the hospital for nine months, even while I kept on with the farmwork all the time. Unless they had been through it themselves, no one could tell what a hard time I had of it.

In 1949, I had an operation for a stomach ulcer. I had such a hard time of it, that I got one serious illness after another.

We farmed 7 *tan* [about 1³/₄ acres]. After Toshio came back from the war, he helped on the farm for about three years and then he went to work for the Tokuyama Sōda Company (in Tokuyama City, in Yamaguchi Prefecture). Sachiko left to get married too, when she was 22. I got so worked up, thinking to myself that I didn't want Sachiko to have a miserable wedding, just because Dad wasn't with us any more, that I ended up crying every night. It was about the time when you could spend only a certain amount of money due to the economic freeze (the measures accompanying the conversion to the new *yen* in 1946). That made it hard too.

I couldn't manage the farmwork all on my own, so we sold the fields one by one, and now there's only 2 *tan* [about ¹/₂ acre] left. It couldn't be helped, because there was only me to hobble about doing the farmwork.

My youngest boy, Shizuyuki, is looking after me now. He works for Tōyō Kōgyō (in Fuchū, Aki District). Together with my daughter-in-law, Miyoe, we grow vegetables on our 2 *tan* and sell them. Miyoe works hard, so these days I don't have any particular worries.

But it's a nuisance that over these last two or three years, as I've got older, so my legs have gradually got painful. All my life, I've done more than my fair share of work, so it's no wonder that they hurt.

3   Shinayo Dōbara

3 The Great Flood and the Atom Bomb

Shinayo Dōbara

Hanging on to our house as it was washed away

My mother-in-law was already dead, so I didn't have to go with the Volunteer Corps when the atom bomb fell. Besides, Nobuko (the second daughter) was only 9 months old. If it wasn't for that, I wouldn't be talking to you now.

I was born on 22 January 1910. It was a place called Nagatsuka Village, in Asa District (present-day Nagatsuka in Gion) where they grew just a little rice. I had four brothers and sisters. My older brother, Kazuichi, died when the atom bomb was dropped. My older sister, Tsuru, was hurt by the atom bomb as well, and that was why later she had a bad liver and died. They're all dead and I'm the only one left now. After leaving Nagatsuka Higher Elementary School, I went to Misasa Municipal Further Education School and learnt there things like sewing, housekeeping and flower arrangement. My mother died when I was 16.

I got married on 7 April 1930, when I was 20. It was an arranged marriage. When I heard that I was going to marry someone in a place called Nukui, I felt I was going to the other end of the earth, because I'd never even heard of it. I didn't much fancy being a peasant, but it was fate so it couldn't be helped.

My husband was called Tatsunobu and he was perhaps 28. He was a steady worker and didn't waste time on other things. He didn't keep the best of health, but people knew him as someone who hated anything that wasn't fair and honest. My mother-in-law was 52 and was in good health. She died when she was 61.

On the farm, I think we had 1 *tan* 6 *se* [about ²/₅ acre] of paddy fields and 1 *tan* 3 *se* [about ¹/₃ acre] of dry land. In between the farmwork, my husband took on work, laying concrete with a crowd of youngsters, and used to go all over.

Even before the atom bomb was dropped, something really frightening happened to me. There was a great storm in 1943 (20

27

September) and the farmhouse was swept away. . . It happened
before the atom bomb, so I'll tell you about that first. The house and
everything in it was swept away.

About 2 o'clock on that day, the fire brigade put out a warning.
They said:

'The River Furu's embankment might burst, so please get ready
to evacuate.'

But in fact, the embankment burst just after that, and in a flash
the flood came. So there was no bloody warning at all. I grabbed
Hatsuyo (the eldest daughter, aged 3) and put her on my back. I
shouted to the other children, 'Run as quick as you can to Kōmoto's'
(a big house nearby) and they took to their heels with nothing but
the clothes they stood up in. Even while that was going on, the water
was rising all the time and there was nothing anyone could do. My
husband put a ladder up to the roof, and shouted, 'Get up on the
roof quickly.' The rain was slanting down in the driving wind. I didn't
want to leave the house empty-handed but, in the end, I clambered
up the ladder without a thing. The wind almost blew me over, but
my husband reached out and pulled me up.

All the time, the water was swirling about and kept on rising. Even
when I got up on the roof, the storm was so fierce that I couldn't
hear what my husband was saying. I just clung on to the roof for
dear life. While this was happening, the house bobbed up and started
to move with the water. It was carried along for about 300 metres. I
felt more dead than alive. The only reason we escaped with our lives
was that it happened during the daytime. Another 14 houses close to
the embankment were swept away at that time. One old lady was
swept away and she was drowned.

Luckily, we came to a halt about 300 metres downstream when we
got caught up in a fence. Without thinking, I said: 'We're saved,
dear!' The village had turned into a lake. Because we were up on
the roof, we could see for miles. After what seemed like ages, a boat
came along from the direction of Nakachōshi. When I saw who it
was, it was an uncle of ours. He called out:

'Oy! Are you there?'

'Yes! We're over here!'

Then he brought the boat over. The current carried us along, but
he managed to get us up on to the embankment a bit downstream.

Our house had been swept away, so we had to look for somewhere
to live. The house where my mother-in-law had grown up was close
by. They'd all gone to work in Hawaii and the house had been let to

someone else. We knew it was a bit of a cheek, but we asked him to let us have a room and take us in.

After a flood you can't farm the land. Sand from the river had got into the fields and covered all the good soil. The layer of sand was even taller than me. We were at our wit's end until lots of Koreans came and got rid of the sand for us, using hand trolleys. That year we could grow a little barley, but only in those places where the good soil had been uncovered.

After the flood, typhoid broke out. During the winter, a lot of people were taken ill. Our Noboru (the eldest son) was in the fifth year of elementary school. He got typhoid too and died in the isolation hospital on 6 October 1944. That wasn't the end of it. After that, Akira (the third son, aged 9) got pneumonia and died on 25 June 1945. Bad luck never comes singly . . . There was no time to get back on our feet before, the next thing we knew, they'd dropped the atom bomb . . .

The medical card proved that he was alive

On the 6th (the day that the atom bomb was dropped), I didn't have the feeling that anything out of the ordinary was going to happen. But that morning of all mornings, before he left, my husband told me what work to do on the farm. What he said was:

'We've done the last weeding (in the paddy fields), so get on with spreading the nightsoil today.'

I thought it a bit odd, because he wasn't the sort of man to tell me what to do before leaving.

He was fit and well, and he set off early in the morning on his bike, taking our second boy, Hiroshi (aged 10; fourth grade of elementary school) with him. Hiroshi was a pasty-faced lad and was being treated at the Kamei Clinic in Yokokawa. The reason why was that my elder sister (Tsuru) had settled down in Uchikoshi and she had told us: 'Kamei Clinic is good, so get them to look at him.' So my husband had been taking Hiroshi there. He always took Hiroshi on the back of his bike.

That morning, too, he took Hiroshi to the clinic and then carried on to work with the Volunteer Corps. Inside the house, I had stretched out my legs on the *tatami* matting and was suckling Nobuko (who was 9 months old) when there was a flash of light. It seemed to me that, for a moment, everything outside was lit up by a white flash and then there was a noise like a big earthquake. Thinking that a bomb had fallen, I dashed from the veranda into the garden, still holding the baby in my arms. When I looked over towards Hiroshima, there was blood-coloured smoke – looking just like a ball of fire – rising up and billowing out towards the north. Straightaway, I thought to myself that Hiroshima had caught it. The neighbours were saying things like: 'Let's go and see what's happened to Hiroshima.' Everyone was saying this and that, but no one knew what had happened, so all we could do was worry. I had the baby, so all I could do was stay in the house and worry myself sick.

About 11 o'clock, I heard Hiroshi shout 'Mum! . . .' as he got back. There was blood coming from his head. I'd been fearing the worst, so I was amazed to see him come home. 'Oh! You've got back! Oh! You've got back!' I said as I hugged him, and then he burst into tears. I was so happy when I saw Hiroshi that I felt as though I was looking at a Buddha. The wound on his forehead was only a scratch, even though blood was gushing out.

Hiroshi said that he'd been sitting in the entrance hall with my sister, waiting to be examined. There was a flash and then the clinic collapsed. They were buried under the fallen building. My sister was the first to get out and then she saved Hiroshi by pulling him out. They ran with bare feet as far as my sister's house in Uchikoshi and, after a bit of first aid, Hiroshi came home across the hills.

If my sister hadn't been there when it happened, I wonder if Hiroshi would have been saved. I still feel grateful to my sister for that. Hiroshi came back home on his own from my sister's house. In fact, my sister's house was in a terrible state. . . I dare say it's more than 2 *ri* (about 8 kilometres) to our house from there. He did really well to get home. As for my sister, later she got a bad liver and died. It came on because of the radiation she got from the atom bomb. Hiroshi didn't even get radiation sickness and he stayed well. Nowadays, I'm living with him and his wife.

My husband didn't come back. I was worrying about what could have happened to him and then I heard that the neighbours hadn't come back either. I couldn't sleep very much on the night of the 6th.

Generally I'm not very keen on that sort of thing, but somebody said to me on the 7th that there was a woman in Nishihara (in Gion) who was a fortune-teller, so why didn't I go and ask her what had happened. She was a shaman. I'm not the type to believe in that sort of thing but a drowning man clutches at straws, so I set off straightaway. The shaman was an old woman. After saying some prayers that I didn't properly understand, she said to me:

'Your loved one will come back.'

I was so pleased to hear that, and then I came back home.

After getting back, I went to the Agricultural Association (present-day Agricultural Cooperative) to get our ration of rice. While I was there, a person from our village who'd been to Nukushina (in Aki) came over to me and said:

'I saw your old man in Fuchū (in Aki District). He asked me to bring Hiroshi's medical card (issued by the Kamei Clinic) and, since I was asked, here it is.'

When I looked at it, I could see that it really was Hiroshi's medical card that he'd given me. I was so pleased that I said whatever came into my head:

'What sort of state was my husband in? Was he alive? He's alive, isn't he? . . .'

The man said: 'He's been injured, but he's alive all right . . .'

So what the shaman had said turned out to be completely true. I was surprised and happy at the same time. I hurriedly thanked the man, collected our rice ration and went back home. Hiroshi's medical card was all crumpled up. I suppose my husband had thought that unless he got the medical card to us somehow, Hiroshi wouldn't be able to go to the clinic any more and that was why he asked the man to deliver it.

There was a hole in his head 3 centimetres deep

Late on the night of the 7th, one of our neighbours, Kitarō Kōmoto, came back home with his whole body covered in burns. I heard that three people from the Volunteer Corps – Kitarō, my husband and Jisaku Miyake – had been ordered to go to Fujimi. When I popped over to the Kōmotos, Kitarō said to me:

'Has Tatsunobu come back?'

I said: 'Not yet.'

Then he told me: 'We talked it over, and decided to split up and try going separate ways. I didn't see any more of him after we split up. I reckon he must have gone towards Hijiyama.'

When I heard this, I felt sure that my husband would come back alive. But Mr Kōmoto and Mr Miyake both died soon after getting back home.

On the morning of the 8th, two of our relatives came and went off to look for my husband. They told me that they found him among a lot of injured people in the corridor of Yaga Elementary School

(Yaga in Hiroshima). 'He's here! He's here!', they said and when
they went up to him, my husband couldn't say anything, but just
wept with joy. The first thing he said when, after a while, he opened
his mouth, was: 'Did Hiroshi get back? Did he get back? . . .' When
they told him that Hiroshi had got back, he just smiled and didn't
say anything more. Blood was coming from his head and he was
burnt around his neck. He didn't seem quite right in the head. Even
so, I suppose he couldn't help but worry about Hiroshi.

One of the relatives came back and borrowed a bicycle cart from
a neighbour. He went off again and they brought my husband back.
Lots of other husbands didn't come back, but mine did on the 8th
and I was so pleased.

But he was terribly injured. On top of his head there was a big
hole and pus was coming out of it. He had a burn on the back of his
neck and one half of his body had turned a purple colour. Perhaps
he'd been thrown into the air by the blast wave and had crashed
against something. He couldn't tell us what had happened to him, so
I suppose it must have been while he was unconscious. We brought
him into the house and laid him on a mattress, but he didn't say a
word. I made some thin rice gruel and, after I'd fed him, he seemed
a bit better and started to say a few things.

The next day, we put him on the bicycle cart and took him to
Suma Clinic (in Higashino). They cleaned the wound on his head
with peroxide. It was about 2 centimetres across, and when we looked
into it, there was something white at the bottom that could have
been bone or flesh. I dare say it was about 3 centimetres deep.

They gave me some peroxide to wipe away the pus. I bought a big
writing brush for that. I'd get it sodden with the peroxide and kill
the germs inside the hole that way. The brush went into the hole
right up to where the bristles joined the handle. Even when I said to
him, 'Does it hurt?', he didn't say anything. Every day, time and
again, I cleaned out the hole on top of his head.

After we brought him home on the 8th, people kept calling at our
house one after another. There were so many houses where husbands
or daughters hadn't come back, and people kept dropping in because
they all wanted to know if my husband had any news. They told us
about who hadn't come back and who had died.

Somebody told us: 'Did you know, Mr Kōmoto (Kitarō Kōmoto)
died yesterday? . . .'

My husband had been working at the same spot with Mr Kōmoto.
It seemed to me that it was after he heard that Mr Kōmoto had died,

that he started to go downhill. People would call in to see him, and after they'd gone, he'd say in a weak voice:

'I can feel it in my bones that I'm going to die too.'

From about the 10th, you could hardly get a word out of him, but if he did say anything, it would just be: 'I reckon I'm going to die too.' Even when I said to him, 'Don't be silly! You can get better if you want to! . . . ,' he would still say, 'I reckon I'm going to die'. I'd give him water gruel to sip, but he'd lost the will to eat and it would just come dribbling out of his mouth. Again and again, I'd wipe the pus from the hole in his head, but it was so miserable to see him lying there as limp as a rag.

From the middle of the night of the 18th, he didn't utter another word and his breathing started to get laboured. After that he wasn't really conscious. On the 19th, it was just as I noticed that he'd brought up some yellowish stuff on to the *tatami* matting that he breathed his last. It must have been just after 1 o'clock in the morning. Next day, we took his body to the riverside and cremated it. When he died, Hiroshi was 10 and in the fourth year of elementary school, Hatsuyo was 5, and Nobuko was 9 months old. I must have been 33. From the time of the flood, it was really one nightmare after another.

I gave up the allowance

What could I do with such small children on my hands? I gave up the 1 *tan* [about ¹/₄ acre] of dry land that we rented. After that, I just farmed our 8 *se* [about ¹/₅ acre] of paddy fields. That wasn't enough to feed us, so I borrowed a kit for weaving *tatami* matting from my relatives, and night and day I just kept on weaving away. My relatives used to say to me:

'If you make yourself ill, what'll become of the kids?'

I used to tether the baby to a doorpost and then, by working flat out at the piece-work, I'd manage to weave two or three *tatami* mats a day.

One day, the welfare officer came and said I could get an allowance. I couldn't sleep all that night, thinking to myself what to do. I knew that I wasn't very strong and I wasn't a big woman either, so I might easily fall ill and then not be able to work. I couldn't see that there was anything else I could do, so I went ahead and we must have got the allowance for about a year and a half. But I could feel that Hiroshi thought it was shameful, us getting the allowance, so I decided to stop it. So for a while after my husband died, we lived from day to day.

About a year after the atom bomb, a letter came right out of the blue. When my mother-in-law had been alive, she used to help a couple of youngsters in the family called Hajime and Zen Takemoto. Later they went to Hawaii. The letter was from this Hajime. In it, he said:

'They tell me that an atom bomb fell on Hiroshima. Is everything all right with you?'

I couldn't tell him just how hard our life was, so I wrote something along the lines of:

'Our house was washed away in the flood, my husband died when the atom bomb was dropped, and things have been pretty bad, but I'm doing all I can to bring up the children. The only trouble is that the children are short of clothes.'

It really cheered me up when he sent some clothes. After that, he sent us something or other almost every month, and that was a big help.

When I got to be about 40, I gave up weaving *tatami* matting and I started to go to work as a labourer. There were lots of people who'd had the same sort of bad luck as me, so I took the plunge and said to some of them:

'If you'll go out to work, I'll go with you.'

I used to tie Nobuko on my back, or else I'd let her play on the site . . . I worked on construction jobs, like the one when they extended the playground at Sanyō Middle School in Motomachi. It must have been against the rules to take children to the site, but the foreman shut his eyes when I took Nobuko along with me, and that was a big help.

When there weren't any labouring jobs, I'd do farmwork. I'd tether Nobuko to a doorpost inside the house and then I'd go and work outside. You see, there wasn't anybody else at home and I didn't have a child-minder. When I'd get back, she'd often be lying face down where she'd cried herself to sleep. On her cheek there'd be the pattern of the mat, looking as though it had been printed there.

It never crossed my mind, but sometimes people said to me: 'If you didn't have kids, you could get married again.' But with three of them, there was never a chance.

Nowadays, I go to the doctor in Hiroshima with Mrs Yokomaru (Tsuyuko Yokomaru). I've got pains in my hips . . . The doctor calls it something like a functional disorder of locomotion, but it never gets any better. Hiroshi works for Mitsubishi Precision Engineering. I'm happy now, living in this house with him and his wife, Kiyoko, and my two grandchildren.

4 Fujie Ryōso

4 We Found His Testament
Fujie Ryōso

My husband didn't come back

I was born on 7 January 1910 into a farming family in Kuchita Village (present-day Kōyō), in Asa District, on the other side of the river. I'll be 71 this year.

When I was a kid, we grew a lot of hemp. In 1926, I took the ferry across the River Ōta, took the road through the mulberry fields, and arrived here to get married. My husband was called Wataru and he was 25 when we got married. The farm had 4 *tan* [about 1 acre] of paddy fields and 3 *tan* [about ³/₄ acre] of dry land, and we raised lots of silkworms. We raised so many silkworms that we kept them in the farmhouse, in the out-house, and wherever else we could, so that there was barely enough room for sleeping.

There used to be a boat that went along the River Furu for collecting nightsoil, though I never went on it. I think it must have been about 1944, when they were making a lot of fuss about increasing food production, that we pulled up the mulberry trees and started to grow things like onions. We sowed all the paddy fields too, with barley as a winter crop. Nowadays, people grow a lot of Hiroshima greens. In those days, we used to call them Kyō greens, but we didn't grow enough to have any left over to sell. All year long, we were busy about the farm. My husband was a kind-hearted man and we used to work really hard.

On the day when the atom bomb fell, we had breakfast just after 6 o'clock. At breakfast time, my husband always used to tell me what sort of work was due to be done during the day, but on that morning of all mornings he didn't tell me a thing. I didn't ask him either what I ought to do that day.

For the last three days, my husband had been going off with his horse and cart to work on dismantling buildings in Hiroshima. He'd planned to bring home a load of old timber. That morning, he said he'd go by bike. He said he was going to give some things as payment to the people at the house where they'd been letting him keep his bike, and so he fixed a bagful of potatoes and onions on to the back

37

of the bike. Then he set off cheerfully. I thought to myself: 'He didn't tell me which jobs need to be done today. I wonder what I ought to do?' What I decided was that I'd go and do some work in the millet field.

I was tending the crops, doing things like weeding, when I made out a B29 flying in from over beyond Hiroshima. B29s would often fly over and I was wondering whether this was another one when, as I looked, it left a trail of smoke behind it. At that very moment, I heard a loud noise from the direction of Hiroshima. A moment later, it was as though the earth shook and a fierce wind sprang up. When I looked over towards Hiroshima, a great cloud of smoke billowed up. That was what afterwards people called the mushroom cloud. Thinking to myself that something terrible must have happened, I rushed back to the house almost on all fours. Inside the house, doors had crashed down and everything was in an awful state. Grandma (mother-in-law) had been looking after two of my kids, but when I got back to the house, she was crouched in a corner of the back room, clutching the kids to her, and saying: 'Oh, my god! Oh, my god!' My youngest (Miyoko) was 8 months old and my other girl, Kazuko, was 2. Our second boy, Takeo, was in the fourth year of elementary school.

Even though I guessed that what had done it was the wind that had hit me in the millet field (the blast wave), I couldn't really make head or tail of it. I stacked up the doors that had crashed down, and it struck me that the house was open to the elements. I said:

'I wonder if that B29 dropped some sort of big bomb? Do you think Dad and Masaru (the eldest son) are all right?'

I couldn't do anything with myself, what with worrying if my husband and Masaru were safe. I couldn't help fearing the worst.

Close to noon, word started to get around that something terrible had happened to Hiroshima. People were saying that Hiroshima was a sea of fire and that it looked as though many people had been killed. I was like a cat on hot bricks, but there wasn't a thing I could do.

It was turned 4 o'clock when our eldest boy, Masaru, came into the house, calling out: 'Mum, I'm back!' All I could say was: 'You've done well to get back! You've done well to get back!' His hands and face, and his legs too, were caked with dirt, and his clothes were in tatters.

Masaru was in the third year at the Shūdō Middle School (in Hiroshima). He was a hard-working lad and, from the time when the pupils had been mobilised, he'd been working in a factory. He told me that at 8.15, when the atom bomb was dropped, he was already inside the factory, waiting to start work. He said that when it happened, some of his friends were still playing about outside the factory and that they were thrown into the air by the blast wave. They'd all been scorched by the flash from the bomb and were dead now. From about the time when Masaru got back home, burnt and blistered people came streaming along the road from Hiroshima. I kept wondering if Dad was all right. I kept going out into the yard to take a look, but he didn't come back.

When night came on, the air-raid warning sounded again and again. Normally, as soon as it sounded, we'd rush out into the air-raid shelter which we'd dug in the yard, but that night I didn't budge. I just kept sitting in front of the household altar to the Buddha. Grandma and the kids didn't feel like going into the air-raid shelter either. We were all worrying whether Dad was safe, so none of us was thinking of saving his own skin. But Masaru kept on putting his hand on my shoulder and saying, 'Mum, let's go into the air-raid shelter', so in the end I did what he asked and went into the shelter. I didn't want to get up from where I'd been kneeling in front of the altar, though . . .

The night was hot and close, and it wore on with the air-raid sirens first sounding the all-clear, and then another warning, over and over again. Grandma kept on chanting away, kneeling in front of the altar and praying to Amida Buddha. I suppose she felt that the only way she could ease her mind was to chant to Amida Buddha. Late in the night, Grandma broke the silence to comfort me, saying:

'Dad knows Hiroshima like the back of his hand, so he's bound to make it back home.'

Those few words set my mind at rest. All the same, I stayed up all night and didn't get a wink of sleep, praying with all my heart and waiting for my husband to come back.

My mother-in-law kept my spirits up

I stayed up all night, but my husband didn't come back. I said:

'Grandma, I'm going to search for Dad, so please look after the kids.'

She said: 'I'm sure he'll come back . . . But if you think it's best to go, of course I'll look after the kids.'

Even so, I couldn't go and leave behind the baby. She was only 8 months old and I was still feeding her. I strapped her to my back and set off. It was dawn and I walked as fast as I could for 2 *ri* (about 8 kilometres) along the road to Yokokawa. At the roadside, there were people who were charred all over or had their skin hanging off. They were squatting down, groaning and asking for water.

As I got close to Hiroshima, the air-raid warning sounded again and again. Every time, I'd look for an air-raid shelter and take cover. The shelters were full of charred people. They were pressed up against each other and groaning. It was like something out of hell. I remembered that my husband had said that he'd be dismantling houses round Nakajima Shinmachi (the present-day Peace Memorial Park). Picking my way across the scorched earth, where everything looked like a picture of hell, I finally made it to the River Motoyasu. At the riverside there were lots of dead bodies piled up. In the river, charred bodies were floating about, bobbing up and down. It was just like hell again.

Among the burnt ruins, there were people who were still alive. In their agony, you could hear them calling out over and over again: 'Mum! . . . Mum! . . .' Thinking that my husband might have tried to get away from Hiroshima in the direction of the Koi Hills, I walked along the railway line. When I crossed the railway bridge at Koi, I was trembling with fear; it was like taking my life in my hands. But there was no other way to cross the river because all the other bridges had burnt down.

My husband wasn't in Koi either. There was nothing more I could do, so I gave up and went home. All day long, the baby just stayed quietly on my back and didn't cry at all.

The next day I set out to search for my husband again. When I got into Hiroshima, I took a different road from the day before and searched here and there for my husband, but I couldn't find him. On the third day, I went looking for my husband as far as the River Motoyasu. They'd let out lots of prisoners, who were dragging bodies out of the river on to the embankment. Every time they pulled a body out of the river and dropped it down, it would hit the ground with an awful thump. Sometimes, as they grabbed an arm to pull out a body, the slimy skin would peel off and the body would drop back into the water with a plopping sound . . . Searching for my husband, I went back and forth, bending over the dead bodies that they'd pulled out of the river, to get a better look at them. Among the bodies, there were two from Kawauchi Village. When I got back to the village, I told their families. One of them was the girl from the house next door to mine. Her body was leaning against the sloping bank of the River Motoyasu. But although some people were found, my husband wasn't one of them.

Day after day, I kept at it, searching through the piles of bodies which they'd pulled out of the River Motoyasu. With my baby strapped on my back, I must have picked over those bodies for about six days in all. I wonder how many tens of thousands of bodies I checked as I walked about? Strange to say, I wanted to find my husband so much that at the time, I didn't feel scared at all. After about seven days had gone by, they said there weren't any more bodies in the River Motoyasu, so I walked about in the Yoshijima District. I checked all the charred bodies in the trams, but my husband wasn't there.

The bodies of schoolgirls were piled up where they'd died in the fire brigade's water tanks. People would cry out, 'It's our lass!' as they found their daughter's body. Young kids of about middle-school age were squatting on the road, or had been laid out on straw mats, and were moaning 'Mum! Mum!' or 'Water, water . . .' All of them were charred black. They were moaning 'Water, water', but there was nothing I could do. When I look back on it now, it was as though I'd become as hard-hearted as a devil.

When people said, 'My husband turned up in such-and-such a refuge centre', or else, 'He's dead, but at least we've found him', I couldn't help being envious. I thought to myself: 'Whatever happens, I've got to find my husband.' So as soon as it turned light, I'd strap the baby on my back and set off for Hiroshima. Once there, I'd just walk round and round. I'd walk over the burnt wastes until I got tired. Hugging my baby, I'd look across the rubble of Hiroshima and wonder where on earth my husband could be.

After ten days or so, I got to thinking that maybe he was alive somewhere, or that maybe he'd already got back home. 'I must get back home quickly and see . . .' I'd think to myself. Even though the sun would still be high in the sky, there were times when I'd stop my searching and go home, with a voice in my heart calling out all the way: 'Dad, Dad!' But my husband wouldn't be there, and sometimes I'd fall down, all of a heap, in the entrance hall. Neighbours would tell me, 'There was someone there who really looked like your husband', and I'd dash off straightaway. But it would be someone else. Time and again I was disappointed.

A lot of the neighbours' husbands didn't come back either. As time went by, I'd sometimes go out searching with them. Friends would come and say: 'What shall we do today? Shall we give it a rest, or shall we go?' Grandma would say to me, 'Take a rest today', but I'd pull myself together and go out searching.

Grandma was a very understanding person. If I took a rest from searching, she'd go in my place. Almost every day Grandma would encourage me, saying:

'It's a good thing that you're still alive to bring up the kids. It's a shame that Wataru hasn't come back. You and me – we both miss him. But we've got to live on, without losing heart.'

Because Grandma was there, I found the strength to go on living and manage the farmwork.

His testament kept me going

Every evening, I couldn't help but feel that my husband was coming back. I'd be weeding the fields and then I'd get the feeling that a voice might suddenly say from behind me: 'Oy, I've come back . . .' When night came on, I'd get this overpowering feeling that he was sure to come back. If there was a noise outside in the middle of the night, I'd rush out straightaway. The children would get a shock to see me suddenly rush outside. But I couldn't help dashing out whenever I thought I heard the sound of my husband's footsteps.

After quite a long time had passed, Masaru would say, 'Dad won't come back now' when he saw me dash outside because of some noise or other. Grandma would say too: 'I don't think he'll come back now.'

But whatever anyone says, I still live in hope that my husband will come back. I'm turned 70 now, but even so, if I hear a noise outside in the middle of the night, my heart starts pounding, thinking that he's come back. People say, 'You should forget your husband now', but I can't forget him. It's unfeeling of them to ask me to forget a husband who disappeared without trace on the day that the atom bomb was dropped. Even now I remember him as though it were yesterday. The older I get, the clearer become my memories. You can laugh at me for being a silly woman, if you like.

There were times when I couldn't help thinking about my husband, even in the middle of doing the farmwork. So the next day, I'd set off for Hiroshima. Even after one or two months had gone by since the atom bomb was dropped, the same feeling would come over me again and again. We'd been growing cucumbers in the fields, but that summer and autumn my heart wasn't in anything except searching for my husband. So the cucumbers that year all died. We had a funeral, but there was no body or anything. Even so, I thought that we ought to bury something of my husband's and when I searched through the house I came across something I hadn't expected in the drawer under the household altar. I found his testament, written on a scrap of paper that he'd torn off a cement bag; and some of his hair and nail clippings were there too. It was sad not to have even one of his bones to bury, but at least we could put his hair and nail clippings into the grave.

I've no idea when it was that my husband wrote his testament. If you'd like to see it, I'll get it out. I've never shown it to anyone else outside the family. I always keep it in the same drawer of the altar where my husband put it. Here it is:

Testament

To the whole family:
1 Bring up the children so that they grow into people whom the country can be proud of.
2 Strive to increase production with all one's might. Never be late in paying our taxes, in kind or in money.
3 Divide up the property fairly. All of you, get on well together.
4 Show respect for the dead, and never disgrace the family's name.

Wataru

He'd put this testament into an envelope that he'd made himself out of a cement bag. On it was written: 'Important! Only to be opened in the event of my death.' He'd folded it over twice and then put it in the envelope. It's been neatly written with a brush, hasn't it? I suppose he thought that, since we were at war, he might die at any time and that he always had to be ready for that. When the atom bomb was dropped, he was 43. He must have written his testament and hidden it in the altar so that he'd be ready whenever his call-up papers came. When I think about how he must have felt, I can't help being moved.

I thought it was a good thing that the testament wasn't addressed to me. In actual fact, my husband might have written it with me in mind, but I can understand what made my husband write 'To the whole family'. It's 36 years since my husband disappeared without trace in the atom bombing. All that time, I've lived the way the testament told us to. Or perhaps I should say that I think it's this testament that's given me the strength to live on.

Between the end of 1945 and early 1946, the men who'd gone to war came back to the village. But my husband, who didn't even go to war, was killed by the atom bomb and he never came back. On nights when I couldn't sleep, I'd often clutch his testament in my hands and soak my pillow.

I tell my grandchildren how cruel war is

I'd go along to the temple too. I'd listen to the priests telling us in their sermons that we ought to resign ourselves to what had happened, or that it was all karma. While I was there, I'd listen to them and think that they were right, but after I got back home, I'd get to thinking about my husband again. All the same, gradually I started to think that if I carried on like that, I wouldn't be able to keep a roof over our heads . . . Grandma was a very wise and considerate old lady and it was thanks to her that I managed the farmwork. I had to feed four kids. It was a time when food was in short supply, so I couldn't afford doing nothing but crying.

As soon as day broke, I'd go out into the fields. I did the washing during the dinner hour. Grandma did the cooking and looked after the kids, so that left me free to concentrate on the farmework. I used to work till about 12 o'clock at night. Except for when I'd had my babies, I'd hardly ever lain down during the day. My health was good, so that's why I could cope with the farmwork. Two of the four kids on my hands were very young. I was still suckling my younger daughter when my husband was killed. Neither she nor her older sister could remember their father.

My oldest boy, Masaru, helped me a lot. However tired I was, and however irritable, I never once smacked the kids. I'd remember my husband and then I wouldn't feel like raising a hand to them. I'd say all sorts to them but I never smacked them. I would have made myself ill if I'd done everything single-handed, so I got them to help with the work . . .

My husband was Grandma's only son. 'I'll do my son's share of the work', she used to say, and she helped me a lot.

Masaru was in the third year at Shūdō Middle School (former system) and the time for him to leave was drawing near. One night, I was lying half asleep when Masaru came and said:

'Mum, please let me go on to university.'

I couldn't give him an answer straightaway. Whichever way you looked at it, I couldn't manage all of our 1 *chō* [about 2¹/₂ acres] of land just on my own. I couldn't decide what to do. The next day, I rushed over to my parents' house in Kuchita Village and talked it over. They said:

'If he wants to go to university, let him go . . .'

I came back with a heavy tread. That night, I said to Masaru, from the bottom of my heart:

'Don't go to university. Stay on the farm with your Mum. I really couldn't manage on my own. I'm sorry, but . . .'

Masaru wanted to become a teacher. It seems that he'd talked about it with his teachers at Shūdō Middle School too. But just before he left school, I heard that his main teacher said to him:

'A farmer should stick to farming.'

Masaru did what I asked and became a farmer for me.

About ten years after my husband died, I bought another 3 *se* [about ¹/₁₃ acre] of land. In those days' money, it cost ¥60000. It's the land where we've got the greenhouse now. It's the biggest thing I ever did. After some time, Masaru took over the farm and he married a girl called Eiko. I'm pleased to see them doing so well on the farm now.

If we hadn't been farmers, I don't know what would have become of our family. I think the soil is something we should really be thankful for. It heals our sorrow and anger, and brings us joy. Mind you, I couldn't have done the farmwork if Grandma hadn't been there to look after my youngest baby. Even though it was a time when food was in short supply, I never let my kids feel they were going without.

I always wanted my kids to grow up right. Each of my four kids grew up just as I wanted them to. They've all grown up and got their own houses. They've all got children. So what more could I ask?

When my grandchildren come at the *Bon* Festival or New Year, I always tell them how cruel the atom bomb was and how frightening war is. They don't really listen . . . but all the same, I tell them the same thing over and over again. 'War is really cruel; it's really cruel. Never make war!' I say to them.

When my grandchildren get a bit bigger, I think I'll show them my husband's testament as well. Or would it be better not to show them? I wonder if it would be best for me to die keeping it to myself? What do you think . . .?

5   Kiyono Fujioka

5 The Mother Who Lay Down with a Corpse

Kiyono Fujioka

My husband and daughter were missing

When they see me, everyone says that I don't look 84. I've been going to the eye clinic, and the doctor said to me:

'Are you still working in the fields? You should take it a bit easier.'

But I told him: 'If I don't go into the fields, I won't be able to farm any more.'

I was born on 7 February 1897. I'm turned 84 now and I'm thankful to still have my health. The place where I was born was Shimomachiya, in Miiri Village, in Asa District (present-day Kabe). We were peasants. There were four of us kids. I had an older brother and sister, so that made me the second girl. When I was 20, I married Tatsujirō. He was five years older than me. We had 6 *tan* [about 1¹/₂ acres] of dry land here, and 2 *tan* [about ¹/₂ acre] of paddy fields. Altogether, that made 8 *tan*, so it was a big farm.

We used to grow crops like hemp, the indigo plant, millet, barley and sweet potatoes. We'd thresh the barley with a simple machine called a *senba*. We used to grow vegetables like *mouli*, but we didn't grow so many as people do nowadays. We ate a lot of millet dumplings. Another thing we used to do was pick the young mugwort shoots and put them into rice cakes. In the old days, we'd pound the rice in a mortar, using our feet. After pounding the rice, we'd lay down straw matting in a big room and spread out the rice cakes to dry. Some of the rice cakes we'd keep in a barrel full of cold water and that way they'd last so that we could keep on eating them right through till spring.

In the dry fields, we turned over the soil by hand with our hoes. Sometimes, on moonlit nights, we'd take lighted lanterns and work in the fields. We'd hang up a lantern at one end of the field and work towards it, digging the furrow as we went. When we'd done that, we'd hang up the lantern at the opposite end of the field and work back towards the light.

47

Tatsujirō was the second son but, all the same, he took over from his father as head of the family. His older brother had gone to work in Hawaii. It was a time when there were all sorts of rumours about people going to America and coming back after making a fortune.

Because he'd got an older brother in Hawaii, it wasn't formally decided when we got married that Tatsujirō would take over as head of the family. Five years after we got married, his parents gave us ¥3000 and said:

'Your older brother is in Hawaii and since he might come back, you go and set up in business somewhere.'

We went to Kure and started a business there, but things didn't work out too well. We already had two kids at that time. Two years later, his parents asked us to come back and, since it didn't look as though his older brother would come back from Hawaii, we left Kure and came back here. After that, we worked really hard on the farm.

When my husband was killed by the atom bomb, he was 55. I was 50.

Early in the morning of the 6th, while I was doing the cooking, my husband made a pair of *ashinaka* straw sandals (straw sandals with a sole for only the front half of the foot). It was a time when footwear was in short supply, so he went off with the Volunteer Corps, wearing *ashinaka*. My husband said to me:

'Today, Chieko (the third daughter; aged 22) is coming too, so you'd better add some barley to the rice when you cook it.'

When I was packing their lunch boxes, I did my best to pick out the rice for them and leave the barley in the pot. After seeing off my husband and daughter, I gathered a load of cucumbers and was bringing them back to the cartshed round the back when it happened. A B29 circled two or three times in the sky above Nishihara. Then there was a big BANG. Because I was in the shade, I didn't notice the flash of light very much. I thought that some sort of bomb must have been dropped over by the elementary school. A parachute floated gently in the sky above the river, moving in an upstream direction. When I got back home, I saw that the house was full of soot. All the doors had crashed down too. I couldn't understand it at all.

In the evening, word came round that we should get mattresses ready and be prepared to go and collect the injured. Other people were saying that the Volunteer Corps had been wiped out. I couldn't find out anything about what had happened to my husband and daughter. I felt like crying, but even tears wouldn't come. I remembered how, in the house that morning, my daughter had been looking in the mirror before she left with the Volunteer Corps. Her eye had caught mine, but she hadn't said anything. That must have been her way of saying goodbye. It was really heartbreaking.

Squabbling over a body in the square at night

Let me tell you about my daughter, Chieko, first. She'd been employed by Mitsubishi Shipbuilders, but she gave that up and was working on the farm. That's how she came to be called out with the Volunteer Corps.

On the night of the 6th, one of the villagers came to tell me:
'Your daughter has made her way back as far as the square at Gion. She's still alive and she was saying: "Please bring some cucumber and barley tea for me." She was calling out, "Mum! Mum!", so please go quickly to her.'

I spread some straw matting on the cart and set off to collect her. In the dark square, dozens of burnt and blistered people were lying around. There was a terrible noise of people groaning. The Ushida Hills were still burning bright red.

Searching by candlelight, I came across someone and thought: 'This is Chieko!' But all of them were burnt, so it was hard to be sure. I touched her burnt and swollen body. She'd stopped breathing, but her body still seemed warm.

Just then, a man pushed me aside from behind. Bending over the body, he said:
'This is my daughter!'

She was burnt all over, but the belt holding up her *monpe* trousers was still there. I couldn't say that it was definitely Chieko's, because it was burnt and had changed colour. After a while, the man went off with the belt, saying:
'I'll go and show it to my family.'

He wasn't sure either. Hours went by as I waited for him to come back. In the end, the man came back and said:
'I showed it to my family, but they say it's not our daughter's.'

He gave the belt back to me. It was about 1 o'clock in the morning of the 7th.

In that dark, hellish Gion square, that man and I had squabbled over a body. Nothing as upsetting as that had ever happened to me before.

I believed that the body was Chieko's, so I brought it back on the cart. It was the middle of the summer, so everywhere people were in a hurry to cremate the bodies. I dressed her in a summer *kimono* and laid her down in one of the rooms. My husband didn't come back. The wife of the priest from the Jōgyō Temple chanted a sutra over Chieko for us and when evening came we cremated the body by the riverside. I tended the fire myself and all the while I kept on praying to Amida Buddha. While the body was burning, I kept on thinking how sad it all was, and how cruel it all was, but the tears wouldn't come. I was shattered.

One week before she died, we'd arranged a meeting for Chieko with a man who was looking for a wife. He was from Saijō in Kamo District (present-day Higashi Hiroshima) and my husband had brought him from Hiroshima on the back of his bike. He was a schoolteacher. But the next day he'd received his call-up papers and he'd gone off to the war. In a letter to us, he'd written:

'There's no knowing what might happen to me now, so it's best for your daughter to forget that we ever met.'

That teacher didn't die in the war and afterwards he came to our house and said:

'I've been demobbed, so now I'd like to marry Chieko.'

I told him: 'Chieko was killed by the atom bomb . . .'

That's the way the world is.

His slimy corpse with the skin peeling off

Next I'll tell you about my husband, Tatsujirō. He was dismantling the buildings at Seigan Temple, in Nakajima, in Hiroshima. He was inside one of the buildings. It seems that the people outside were on fire and that they jumped into the river straightaway. That's why so many bodies were never found. Some must have been washed out to sea and others must have sunk to the bottom of the sea, so they were never found.

They brought my husband's body back by boat up the River Ōta on the 7th. There was a piece of paper attached to his body with Tatsujirō Fujioka written on it. Perhaps his clothes had all been burnt, because he was stark naked. His skin was slimy and peeling off, but he wasn't charred. There was a big hole – as much as 5 centimetres across – in his head. A length of timber, or something like that, must have fallen on him, I suppose. He was burnt, but because he'd been indoors, his body was still in one piece.

I took the cart and went to the river jetty at Takase (in Kawauchi, in Satō) to collect his body. Then I brought him back home. I put a *kimono* on him and laid him down in the room where the household altar is. His burnt and ulcerated skin gave off such a nasty smell that it's hard to describe it . . . You know what I mean – that peculiar sort of smell.

I'd already brought back my daughter's bones from the riverside and put them into a pot that I'd placed in the altar. Now I laid out my husband in front of the same altar and sat with him.

Grandma (mother-in-law) and I had to chant the sutras together under a dim light because of the air-raid precautions. It got late and as I was getting ready to sleep, Grandma – who was 80 years old then – said:

'Tonight I'll sleep beside Tatsu. It's the last chance I'll have to be with him.'

That was how she asked me to let her sleep beside my husband. It was something that hadn't even entered my head.

Grandma lay down next to my husband, inside the same mosquito net. As I was hanging up the mosquito net, I was quite overwhelmed, thinking about how deep the affection is between parents and children. It must have been really smelly; it was such a terrible stench. But even so, Grandma didn't so much as stir all night long. I was really grateful to her for lying with my husband.

On the 8th, I was busy from early morning, getting ready for the cremation. We took my husband to the spot where the day before we'd burned our daughter's body and cremated him there. At that time, there was only a handful of houses where they'd got their husbands' bodies back. I felt I was lucky just to get my husband's body back. All the same, thinking that death had taken my husband away, I clenched a handful of sand from the riverside as I watched his body burning.

When the war ended, my husband's younger brother – Kazuto – and his family came back from Korea. Everything they had was in one rucksack, and they brought with them their three children. This livened up the house, but in the evenings I'd be beside myself with sadness and I'd start to cry. If I went back to the house, Kazuto's wife would be there. I didn't want to let her see that I'd been crying. I used to pretend that I was still clearing up after work, but in fact I was often having a cry outside. In the barn, I'd cry until I could cry no more, and then I'd go into the house.

In those days, we weren't growing vegetables for sale. We grew potatoes of one sort or another, and barley too, and had to deliver them to the authorities. It wasn't easy to feed the family.

It was a big help that, after the war, my oldest boy, Tatsuo, was soon demobbed. Even now, we live off the land as farmers and don't have any other jobs. We grow vegetables on 6 *tan* [about 1$^{1}/_{2}$ acres] and last year we put it all under Hiroshima greens.

People have always said that when there's a slump, it leads to war. I hope that there won't be any more wars. When my great-grandchildren get to be 20, war could well break out and then the time might come again when people are killing each other. When I think about it, it scares me, the way things are going now. There mustn't be another war. There mustn't.

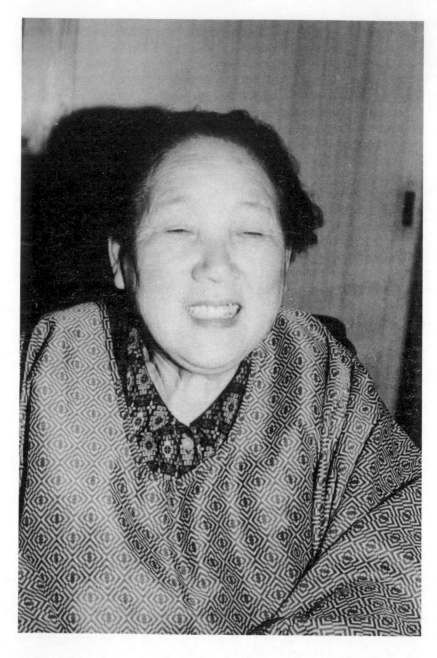

6 Tamano Momoki

6 A Coffin Made from Medicine Chests

Tamano Momoki

They cremated our daughter on a sheet of metal

My parents' house was in a place called Tonoga in Yamagata District (present-day Kake) and I was born on 27 October 1906. I'll be 75 this year.

My husband was called Masaichi and he was 48 when he was killed by the atom bomb. My husband and I got married in 1935. He'd got two children from his first marriage. My husband was in the medicine trade and he was the sort of man who got on well with everybody he met. The old Grandad next door lingered on for ten days after he was injured by the atom bomb, but he said:

'Mr Momoki was such a good person. If even people like him are dying, then someone like me is bound to die.'

That'll give you an idea of how well he got on with other people and how people liked him. When he was at home . . . well, perhaps I needn't go into all that.

He used to sell his medicines over a wide area. He'd got a factory and a wholesaler's store in Midorii, and he had a couple of salesmen. He did business as far afield as Mie Prefecture. Sometimes he used to send off his medicines by boat. I used to help him with his business as well as working in the fields.

When they dropped the atom bomb, our boy, Tsuyoshi, was 4. Our eldest girl, Miyoko, was 24. Our second girl, Yukie, was 18. And our third girl, Sanae, was 6. You didn't have to go with the Volunteer Corps if you had children under 3. The people in charge kindly pretended that Tsuyoshi was still tiny. That's how I came to be at home and wasn't killed. My husband and two stepdaughters, Miyoko and Yukie, went off to Hiroshima with the Volunteer Corps and were there when the atom bomb fell.

On the morning of the 6th, I was at home making *umeboshi* pickles. I was just putting down a jar when a blinding flash made me jump. The doors and *shōji* screens were all sent flying . . . It was getting

55

towards evening time when Miyoko came back. She'd gone with the Volunteer Corps to Mitsubishi's (at Kannonmachi in Hiroshima) and thank goodness she got back safely. Miyoko said:
'It's terrible in Hiroshima.'
All the same, I didn't go out searching for my husband on the 6th, because I still thought he'd be coming back.
It was early on the morning of the 7th that someone told me: 'Mr Momoki is at Yutani . . .'
I rushed there straightaway. Someone there told me:
'If it's Mr Momoki you're looking for, a few minutes ago he was nattering away.'
I went to look and found my husband among a crowd of injured people, all of them charred black.
I called out to him: 'I've come, dear!'
But he was dead already. I suddenly remembered the way he'd said, as he left the day before:
'Our kids are still small, so I can't afford to get killed in an air raid.'
I shouted: 'Dear! I've come, dear!'
But strange to say, the tears wouldn't come. I suppose I was too shocked, and anyway it was like being in the middle of hell with all those injured people around me . . .
Miyoko and me carried him outside and put him on the cart. We covered him with a *kimono* that I'd brought with me and took him home. After getting back home, I was going to wipe his body with a towel, but when I touched him, his slimy skin peeled off . . . so I gave up. All he'd got on were his pants and one *chikatabi* plimsoll. There was nothing we could do about his black, charred body. Clutched in both hands were bits of skin, like wood shavings, which had peeled off his body. No one can say what he must have gone through. We broke up several medicine chests and made a coffin out of them. Then we carried it to the riverside and cremated him.
On the 8th, the neighbours looked after the children for me and, taking Miyoko with me, I went to search for Yukie. She had died close to the River Motoyasu. One of the rescue teams had piled up four or five bodies on a sheet of metal and they were getting ready to cremate them. Among the bodies was Yukie's.
One of the men in the rescue team said:
'She was a pretty girl.'
Her dead body was burnt and swollen like a boiled octopus, but

her face hadn't altered very much. They cremated her for us on the metal sheet.

I'm sorry to change the subject, but 13 years ago (in 1968) a person from over Kabe way told me that in the memorial tower, in the Peace Memorial Park, there were the remains of an atom bomb victim and that written on them was 'Yukie Momoki'. But Yukie was definitely cremated by the side of the River Motoyasu. One of the men in the rescue team did it for us, while Miyoko and me looked on. After he'd done it, we collected her bones and brought them home. I thought it was strange, but when someone tells you about the remains of your daughter, you can't just ignore it. So I went along to the memorial tower. Inside a box, there was some hair. There was no mistaking that written in pen on the rough cedar wood was 'Yukie Momoki'. The name of the person who had cremated her was written down too. He was from Yamaguchi Prefecture. I brought the box home and we put the cloth that the box had been wrapped in, together with the hair, into Yukie's grave.

On the 9th (August 1945), Miyoko went off to Hiroshima to help look for Kimie Neishi from next door. I gave her some cigarettes that we had in the house to take with her and told her to give them as a thank you present to the man from the rescue team who'd cremated Yukie the day before, if she ran into him. Unfortunately, though, she came back without seeing him. Kimie from next door often used to come to our house to use our sewing machine. They found her body and they knew it was Kimie by the pattern on a scrap of material stuck to it. That was from some pants that she'd made for herself at our house.

Hard for mother and hard for the children too

So I became a widow, with two kids – aged 4 and 6 – to look after, and a daughter who was ready for marriage. For a while, we managed to live on the money that my husband had saved from his medicine business, but soon the money ran out. Then a friend of ours in Furuichi took some of our stock of unsold medicines and went off into the mountains (the farming villages in the mountainous district of Western Chūgoku) to sell them door-to-door. Another thing we did was barter some of the medicines for food. That's how we managed to support ourselves for a while longer. But there were controls on selling medicine and there was the economic freeze too, so it got harder. We could draw from our savings only ¥400 a month for a family of four, so I tried not to waste a single coin.

I went out to work as a labourer, but they paid me only 80 or 90 *sen* a day. Everybody else got ¥1 30*sen*, but because I was 50, I didn't get the full daily rate. About the time when the kids moved on from elementary school to middle school (about 1955), our savings had all run out and things got really hard. By the time the kids were going to high school, there were some months when they needed ¥2000 between the two of them. So whatever the weather, I'd go out labouring every day. There wasn't much food, but we struggled on, living on millet and sweet potatoes. Somehow I managed to feed the kids. At least I didn't let them starve.

There'd be some mornings when I'd wake up the kids after making their packed lunches and then I'd go off to Kannonmachi to work as a reed-cutter. I'd get to Kandabashi in Ushida by 6 o'clock and, before starting work, I'd burn moxa in about 50 places on my arms to toughen them up. I was younger then, so I could stick at it and work hard.

Food was short, so I rented 6 *se* [about ¹/₇ acre] from Mr Hirao (a neighbouring farmer) and started to grow vegetables. When I'd finished work, I'd walk home from Hiroshima. However much I hurried, it would be after 8 o'clock by the time I got home. Then I'd go out into the field to work on the vegetables. It saved money not to have to buy them, so I thought that at least I'd grow my own vegetables . . .

I worked in the field at night. But I didn't want people to think that I was stealing from their fields and I thought it would be miserable for the kids if people said, 'Over at the Momokis, the mother works at night.' So when people passed by, I'd crouch down quietly among the vegetables. Hiding myself away, I was a night-time farmer.

Although I wanted to dress my kids like everybody else's, I couldn't manage it. I let Sanae go to the high school at Kabe, but she had only one skirt. I heard that one of the teachers, who didn't know anything about that, said to her:

'Can't you wash your skirt for once?'

Even though the teacher told her to, I couldn't wash her skirt, because she didn't have a change.

When she went to high school, I said to her:

'We can't manage to be like everyone else, so you'll have to face up to it, that you might have to go to school wearing straw sandals, even if the others are wearing shoes.'

I suppose she understood. She didn't show any particular sign of being upset when she used to go off to school.

When I see people nowadays changing from one set of clothes to another, I remember all the more how hard it was then. You may say that times are different, but people these days have too much. If things carry on as they are now, it will be all right. But generally, there are more hard times than there are easy times in people's lives. I think we ought to know how to put up with things. Sanae understood all this, and she put up with things. She got married 15 or 16 years ago. She bought nearly all of her own trousseau herself. I forgot to say, but our eldest girl, Miyoko, got married in 1946, although I wanted her to stay at home to help me . . .

I'll tell you another thing. I once saw a boy in a shop nearby secretly slipping some sweets into his pocket. I suppose when kids see something they want to eat, and if they don't have any money, they'll steal it. I couldn't do all that I wanted for my kids and it really made me wonder whether, by chance, my kids too might do something wrong. All the other houses round here bought fridges and washing machines. But we couldn't afford them, so it was much later that we got them.

Our house was more than half destroyed in the great flood of 1943. But the firemen raised it up out of the sand for us and in the end we made it livable again.

The flood damage at that time was terrible. The River Furu's embankment was breached upstream of us and the flood went straight through our house. All that we managed to save was what we piled up on a chest of drawers. That was just 100 boxes of ready-for-sale medicine, a Buddhist scripture, the name tablets of the dead, some prayer beads, everybody's nightwear and 2 *shō* [about 3½ litres] of rice. The rest of our furniture was all swept away. It was a good job that it was daytime but, all the same, an old lady and a girl from the village were swept away to their death. We were on the embankment and we saw them swept away, but it was such a flood that there was nothing we could do to help them.

The atom bomb was dropped before we had a chance to get back on our feet after the flood. Because of that, the house was so rickety that you could say it was no more than a roof over our heads. When the rain leaked in, I used to go from one room to the other, putting out buckets and tubs. When the rain was really leaking in, I'd get up on the roof to adjust the tiles. I couldn't afford to feel any shame about it. I used to think that people might be saying about us: 'I wonder how the Momokis manage to stay alive. It's a wonder they don't fall ill.' The more I'd think about that, the harder I'd work, night and day, to feed us all and to bring up the kids.

When we had only 6 *se* [about ¹/₇ acre] of land, we couldn't make much money out of selling vegetables. So I rented another 9 *se* [just under ¹/₄ acre] and started to grow barley and millet. Because we hadn't always been peasants, I had to borrow the tools from the neighbours. They were all good to me, telling me how to grow the crops and even things like how to tie up the spinach leaves.

When Sanae went out to work, she used to go off with the Yokoyamas' daughter, who lived in Nakachōshi. I heard that she said to Sanae:

'Your mother works really hard, doesn't she? Everyone looks up to her.'

It made me really happy. Even after all this time, I'm grateful that she said to Sanae such a nice thing about me.

It's true that I had to work really hard to bring up the kids. It was hard for me as their mother, but it was hard for the kids too. I'm sure you'll understand that the reason I'm telling you about the hard times I had isn't to make my kids feel that they owe me something.

Before my son, Tsuyoshi, got married, I said to him:

'When you were a kid, I couldn't do everything for you that the other parents did for their kids. When you get married, you can live your own life. You don't have to stay here with me . . .'

He didn't say anything, but he had this house built 13 years ago so that I could live with them. Even when times were hard, I did think about getting a little house built for us, but I just couldn't manage it. I'm lucky that now, thanks to my children's hard work, I can live in a nice house like this. Although I was widowed, I've had a long life and now I'm 75. My dead husband lies there under the turf and he's watching over me. I really believe that it's all thanks to the dead. In my heart, I've decided that I'll use whatever life is left to me to say my prayers for him every day.

7 Tsuyuko Yokomaru

7 My Unweaned Baby Was Irradiated Too . . .

Tsuyuko Yokomaru

Clutching my swollen breasts

My parents' house was in Yamamoto in Shimo Midorii. They were farmers who rented their land; what you'd call tenant-farmers. They had about 5 *tan* [about 1¼ acres]. My father died when I was 18. I had five brothers and sisters. I was the eldest girl so I helped my mother, doing jobs like collecting the nightsoil and weaving *tatami* matting. I used to weave about four mats in a day and my mother spun the warp.

We grew rushes too – about 7 *se* [¹/₅ acre] or so. We wove all the rushes that we grew into *tatami* matting. It was a hard life, being tenant-farmers. Most of what we grew, we had to hand over to the landlord. We raised crops like Kyō greens, burdock and Chinese leaves. When the time for the *Bon* Festival drew near, even farmers couldn't get by without money. So mother and I would urge on the younger children and we'd all work together. It was hard work for us all. Up until I was 21, I worked like a donkey in the fields.

My husband and I had an arranged marriage. My husband's elder sister lived over towards Midorii and she was the one who arranged the marriage. My husband was called Masaru and he was 29. He was eight years older than me. He was in the building line of business and they specialised in laying foundations. He was on the short side. He often used to joke: 'You couldn't even make rice gruel out of me.'

What he meant was that there was an old saying that you can't make rice gruel out of 5 *shaku* [勺] of rice. Perhaps you haven't heard it. He was joking, pretending that 5 *shaku* [尺]* meant 5 of the other *shaku* [勺].† Being a small man, my husband wasn't even 5 *shaku* [尺] tall. We were just like a couple of fleas, because they

---

Shaku [尺]: old unit of length; 1 *shaku* = 30.3 cm or about 1 foot.
†*Shaku* [勺] old unit of volume; 1 *shaku* = 0.018 litres.

63

say that with them too the female is bigger than the male.

My husband had three brothers and sisters. When I got married and moved in with his parents, his younger sister, Haruko, and younger brother, Jirō, were still living at home. They did the farmwork, and I worked hard on the farm too, with his old parents. Round here we grew a lot of millet.

Now I'll tell you about the morning of the 6th August. The millet had grown to be 1 or 2 *shaku* [30–60 centimetres] high, so I was thinning it out. I noticed a B29, and was thinking to myself that it was flying over towards Oda, when there was a noise like a big THUD. Over in Hiroshima direction, a big cloud of smoke and flame rose up, looking almost like an enormous beachball twisting round. The burdock in the next field was in full flower. I rushed over there and hid myself for a while, waiting to see what would happen.

When I got back home, I found that the clock had stopped. The *shōji* screens were broken and had crashed down. Things had fallen off the shelves and were lying around all over the place. Suddenly it struck me that something terrible must have happened and that my husband might have been hurt. Kenzō Tochimura from next door had come back from Hiroshima early, with a load of old timber from the dismantled buildings on his horse and cart. I asked him:

'Have our Dad and the others been hurt?'

But his answer was:

'Nothing happened in Hiroshima while I was there. What happened after I left, I don't know.'

When I stopped and thought about it, he'd already got back when I heard the noise like a big THUD, so of course there was nothing he could tell me when I asked him.

About 11 o'clock, a stream of injured people started to come along the road. Thinking to myself that something terrible must have happened, I couldn't stay still. I ran all the way to my parents' house in Shimo Midorii and asked them:

'What do you think has happened?'

But they didn't know anything either.

Meanwhile, word had got around that survivors from the Volunteer Corps were on their way back to the river jetty or Kawauchi Elementary School. I spread a straw mat on the cart and tied on a mattress, before running to the school. But my husband wasn't there. Then people started to say that the survivors were being brought by boat to Shōwa Bridge. I ran there, pulling the cart behind me, but he wasn't there either. I thought to myself that if he was coming by boat, it might be to Takaseguchi (in Kawauchi), so I ran there. But again my husband wasn't there. Evening turned to night and I was still rushing here and there, pulling the cart behind me, but I couldn't find my husband. He wasn't to be found anywhere.

While all this was going on, Old Man Yokochi (Toshiko Yokochi's husband) had come back. I went to see how he was. I wanted to ask him what had happened to my husband and the others, but he was so burnt, he was like a skinned rabbit, and all I could do was stand watching. Dawn came on, with me still thinking to myself that my husband would come back later . . .

Early on the morning of the 7th, I heard that the survivors had got back to Yutani in Gion. I hurried there with the cart. There were a lot of injured people, groaning 'Give me some water, give me some water!' But my husband wasn't among them. People said that the dead had been taken to Shōsō Temple in Gion, so I ran over there. There were charred, dead bodies lying around everywhere. They were covered with straw mats. One by one, I looked under each mat. My husband wasn't there, but Shigeru Sugita (Chiyoko Sugita's husband) and Shinichi Nomura (Masako Nomura's husband) were. While I was checking the dead bodies, the thought struck me that we might have missed each other and that he might be back home. So I hurried back home. My husband hadn't got back, but my mother had come to keep an eye on things while I was out.

At that time, I had five kids. Our eldest boy, Masayoshi, was 15. He'd been called up into the land army and had been working on a farm in Tomo (present-day Numata). But when it happened, he was home on leave. Our second boy, Masaharu, was 13 (and was in the sixth year of elementary school). Our third boy, Hiroshi, was 11 (fourth year of elementary school) and our fourth boy, Seizō, was 6. Youngest of all was our daughter, Kiyoko. She was $1^{1}/_{2}$. As for me, I was 36.

I walked all over, searching for my husband. My breasts would fill with milk. So I'd go back home, feed Kiyoko, and then go out searching again. In desperation, I ran all over, clutching my swollen breasts, and thinking to myself, 'I wonder where he can be lying dead?' or 'I wonder if he's alive somewhere?'

My unweaned baby too was poisoned to death

I suppose it must have been for about ten days that I went on searching. I went to Yokokawa and spent half a day checking all round there. There wasn't a scrap of shade in Hiroshima, as I ran around, wearing *monpe* trousers, with straw sandals on my feet, and a hand-towel on my head to keep off the sun. When I got tired from walking around, I'd sit on the burning hot roadside and think to myself: 'Why can't I find him?' His elder sister and her boy had been burnt, but they got back home. They were badly injured and I treated their wounds with a cold poultice of raw potato.

After about ten days, Kiyoko started to get poorly. I'd got two sick people to look after, and there was my unweaned baby too, so I couldn't get away to search for my husband any more. Jirō (my husband's younger brother) worked at the Japan Steelworks (in Funakoshi) and he said to me:

'I've looked all over for him, but I can't find him either. I think you'll have to give him up for lost.'

Even though he told me that, I still wanted to go out searching for my husband. But with sick people on my hands, there was nothing I could do.

Kiyoko was 1½ and she didn't even cry. She took her milk readily enough, but all the same, day by day, she grew weaker and lost all energy. I took her to Hirano Clinic. It was packed with sick people. After waiting for hours, a doctor eventually took a look at her. As he was giving her an injection, he said to me:

'If this makes her cry, there's some hope for her . . .'

He gave her the injection, but she didn't cry. He asked me:

'Was this child exposed to the radiation?'

I said: 'Because she's still small, I left her at home when I went out searching for my husband, so she wasn't exposed . . .'

The doctor didn't reply.

About the 20th, the soles of her feet got swollen. And on the 24th, Kiyoko died. It was such a short life she had – just over one year. No one could tell what it was she died from. Afterwards, I got to thinking that perhaps it was the radiation that I'd been exposed to, or some sort of poison in my milk, that got into Kiyoko's body and killed her. We made a little box and put Kiyoko into it. We couldn't manage a funeral or anything like that. I took her to the place for cremating bodies and I dug a hole there and burnt her. I was just wearing my everyday *monpe* trousers, which were patched all over
. . .

In the end, my husband didn't come back. I didn't feel like getting on with the farmwork. Towards the end of August, I had a nervous breakdown and got appendicitis. They said to me at Tademoto Clinic in Midorii:

'As soon as you get busy, you'll be back to normal.'

But for about a month, I just mooned about, doing nothing in particular. Towards the end of September, bit by bit, I got into the mood for work again.

My husband had left behind some hair and his nail clippings. Four days before they dropped the bomb, he had given them to me and said:

'If I die, these will stand for me.'

Soon after, he was killed by the bomb and we never got him back in any shape or form, so I suppose he must have had a premonition. We put them into his grave.

It was hard to feed and clothe the kids. Rice was rationed too. Although I had 2 *tan* 2 *se* [just over ¹/₂ acre] of paddy fields, after we'd delivered our quota to the authorities all we had left were the rejects. Can you imagine what it was like trying to feed four growing lads? No wonder I had a nervous breakdown! There wasn't anybody else in the village who had it as hard as I did. Nobody else had the bad luck I've had. I lost my father when I was 18 and my husband was killed by the bomb when I was 36, so my life has been one long struggle.

I sent Masayoshi out to work and they paid him 80 *sen* a day. Before that, I didn't have any money coming in, so it was hard making ends meet. There was nothing else for it but to send him out to work as a day-labourer. I used to go to collect nightsoil, taking our second boy, Masaharu, with me. He was just 13. Sadaichi Nakagawa, Junji Fukunaga and other neighbours of ours used to go with a horse and cart to collect nightsoil from the Railway Training Institute at Mukainada (present-day Hiroshima Railway College). They let me in on their round and, to start with, they used to take me with them. I'd get up about midnight, cook some rice mixed with *mouli*, make it into rice balls, and then set off. It was a full day's work.

Early in 1946, after the war had ended, I remarried, this time to my husband's younger brother, Jirō. But he wasn't with me for long either, because he died in December 1947. We lived as man and wife for less than two years, but during that time Yoshiaki was born. After Jirō died, I had to start collecting the nightsoil again. The cart had iron-rimmed wheels and I used to take three tubs on it to

Mukainada, load them up, and pull it back again. Around Ōzu Bridge there was a vineyard. On the way to Mukainada, dawn still wouldn't have broken. Masaharu used to push from behind, while I pulled the cart, with Yoshiaki on my back. I was still feeding him. On the way back, we'd have our dinner in the shade of the vines and I'd give Yoshiaki my breast. On frosty mornings, the cart would slip a lot, so it was hard work.

I used to keep Masaharu off school when we went to collect nightsoil. He helped me a lot and didn't grumble. We used to make straw sandals at night. Then we'd put them on and set off. We'd wear out two pairs, going to Mukainada and back.

On Sundays, I'd take Masaharu with me and we'd go to Nukui Hill (a wood owned in common by the village) to collect firewood. We had to do it, because we couldn't afford to buy firewood. The children didn't have enough clothes to wear, nor food to eat, and even in winter they had to go without woollens. I had to dress them in rough working clothes all the time. I never put any make-up on my face. Everything went on the children, so there was nothing left for make-up. I used to patch even the patches on my *monpe* trousers.

At times when there was no farmwork to do, I used to work as a builder's labourer for the Takahashi Building Company in Nishi Kaniya. I was a day-labourer. I'm having to pay now for the hard work I did then. I've got pains in my legs and my hips, and it really plays me up. For one thing, I can't bend my right leg at all now.

I didn't want people saying that my son couldn't get married because he had to look after his widowed mother. So we found him a wife in 1958. At long last, I'm free of worries and life's a lot easier. But the pain in my legs and hips is getting worse. Even the doctor says, 'There's nothing much I can do for you', so I don't suppose it will get better. I think it will still be with me when I die and go to meet my husband. On rainy days, it hurts like hell and I don't know what to do with myself. I'm in a right old state.

8   Masako Nomura

8 He Came Back Alive, But . . .

Masako Nomura

He came back by boat

I was born in the year of the monkey – on 7 October 1920. So I'm 60 this year. The place where I was born is now called Kamiyaguchi in Kōyō. I had an elder brother and a younger brother, so there were three of us kids. From Kuchita Elementary School I went on to the Continuation School. As well as helping with the farmwork, I learnt how to sew and do other things. My father was an old-fashioned person and he used to say:

'A young girl shouldn't go out to work.'

So that was why they made me do the work about the house.

There was a go-between who made the arrangements for me to come here. My husband was called Shinichi. He must have been 28. I was 21. It was towards the end of the summer that the go-between came with Shinichi to see me. After that, things went like clockwork . . . In those days, most weddings took place before the harvest. In my case too, I suppose they were in a hurry to get the wedding over.

Within a month of being introduced to him, I was married. At the wedding, I could hardly remember his face or anything about him. I got on the boat at Yaguchi Jetty on the River Ōta and went off to get married. We didn't have a honeymoon or anything like that. It was right in the middle of the autumn harvest, so we were back at work the day after our wedding. My husband was killed by the atom bomb, so we'll have to have our honeymoon after I've joined him in the next world . . .

My husband was a man of few words. He was gentle and kind. He was a good man and people liked him. Although he was on the short side, he was sturdily built. He explained to me that he'd cut off a finger when he was threshing rice. So his index finger on his right hand was as short as this. If he'd gone as a soldier, he couldn't have pulled the trigger on his rifle, so they made him a reservist. He used to say:

71

'There's no knowing when I might be called up . . .'
We must have had 2 *tan* [about ½ acre] of paddy fields and 4 or 5 *tan* [about 1 acre] of dry land. The paddy fields were in Tomotake (present-day Kōyō) on the other side of the river, so I used to row across with my husband to work in those fields. Here (in Kami Nukui) it was just dry land. Even though the big river (the River Ōta) flowed right by us, we couldn't put this land under water. We just had dry fields here and we grew a lot of *mouli*, burdock, millet, potatoes, barley and such like. We were kept really busy.

As the war took a turn for the worse, even when we grew barley and sweet potatoes, they all had to be delivered up to the authorities. My husband used to set off by boat about 1 o'clock in the morning to collect nightsoil from Hiroshima. Whenever he went, I'd get his food ready and go as far as the riverbank at the back of our house to see him off. It might sound quite romantic, but it was nothing like that. At a later stage, he changed to an ox-cart for collecting the nightsoil.

On the morning of the 6th, he went off, saying:
'I should be able to get back early today . . .'
Our Masae had turned 2. She was a sickly child and we often had to take her to the doctor's. On that morning too, I strapped Masae on my back and was on the way to the Hirano Clinic in Yaguchi. I took the ferry across the river and when I was near to Aki Yaguchi Station (on the Geibi line) it happened. I felt a blinding flash, and in the same instant, there was a big BANG that made me jump. I was really startled. I was so shaken up that I couldn't tell whether the flash had come first or the bang . . .

When I got to Hirano Clinic, the glass in the windows had been broken and it was in a terrible state. All the same, the doctor took a quick look at Masae. Then, thinking to myself that something awful must have happened, I hurried home. From the ferry on the way home, I could see black smoke rising up into the sky over Hiroshima. It was enough to make anyone worry. Thinking to myself that it must have been a bomb or something, I got back home and took a look at the house. It was a right old mess. The *shōji* screens were lying about and the Emperor's picture had fallen down. It was terrible!

About 7 in the evening, somebody told me that my husband was on the way back by boat. I don't remember who it was who told me. Taking a summer *kimono* for my husband with me, I went to the riverside at Takase (in Kawauchi Village) and got on the boat, together with Misano Nakaoka, Himeyo Hamamoto and Mr and Mrs

Hamao. After going downstream quite a way, we met another boat coming upstream. A voice called out:
'Shinichi is on this boat . . .'
They pulled over our boat for me, so that I could get on the boat coming upstream. Sure enough, my husband was there. His whole body was covered in burns and his face was pitch black. He was stark naked too. He'd got a torn *chikatabi* plimsoll on just one of his feet. His lips had swollen up to a huge size, so much so that if he hadn't said something, I wouldn't have known it was my husband. While we were on the boat, I put the summer *kimono* on him. When we got on shore, we put him on a wooden board and some people carried him for me from the riverside to our house. I hardly noticed who it was who carried him for me.

After we'd put him on a mattress, he kept on saying, 'Give me some water, give me some water' and 'My belly hurts; it hurts'. Somebody said that the white of eggs was the best thing to use, so I cracked lots of eggs and smeared the white all over his body. But when you're as burnt as he was, smearing with egg-white isn't going to be enough to save you. Although he kept saying, 'It's agony, it's agony!', there was nothing we could do for him. Because he was conscious, he must have suffered terribly. He didn't say so much as my name or a word about our baby.

As a precaution against air raids, we had to put a black cloth around the light bulb. In its dim light, all I could do was watch over my delirious husband, as he kept groaning, 'It's agony'. I think it must have been about 9 o'clock when he breathed his last . . . I dampened a flannel with water and dabbed his swollen lips. Holding Masae in my arm, I closed his eyes for the last time.

Next day, my father came to help me cremate my husband. Setting light to the fire, I felt sorry, now that he was dead, that I hadn't given him a proper drink when he'd kept on moaning, 'Give me some water, give me some water!'

It was hell for those left alive too

For about a month, I was like someone out of her mind and I didn't feel like doing anything. My head just wouldn't work. I tried moxa treatment and other things, but I suppose it must have been the shock of losing my husband, because my head kept on buzzing . . .

I'd got my sick father-in-law living with me, and I wasn't right in the head myself, so life got harder and harder. We were short of money. I was wondering what it would be best to plant for the autumn crop, and it was when I saw the young greens sprouting that suddenly my strength came back to me . . . I'd just decided that I would make a go of things on my own when, on 17 September, there was a flood (the Makurazaki Typhoon) and our fields were washed away. The fields were covered with grit to a depth of about 1 *shaku* (30 centimetres). So what I had to do after that was dig out the good soil (the topsoil) and bury the grit underneath it. I did it all on my own, one spadeful at a time. My father-in-law was an invalid, so he couldn't do a thing to help me. I let Masae play in the fields while I got on with repairing the flood damage.

For about ten years, I was a woman doing a man's work. The flood had made the soil a lot less fertile and we didn't have any fertiliser. We grew *mouli* and carrots, but they were all stringy. Single-handed, I worked the 2 *tan* [about ¹/₂ acre] of paddy fields in Yaguchi too. When Masae was sick, I used to leave her lying down in the house on her own, while I'd go across the river to work in the fields.

If I worked hard on the dry land, the paddy fields would get choked with weeds. On the other hand, if I spent my time in the paddy fields, the dry land would end up covered in weeds. In my heart, I was always grieving, wishing my husband was with me, although I knew that I couldn't bring back the past. My neighbours had all been widowed, so there was nobody who could show me how to do the farmwork. It ended up that when everybody else sowed burdock, I did the same. All I could do was work in the way I thought best. So when the burdock was ready, I'd start work in the middle of the night. I'd work in the dark until dawn, groping my way and rooting up the burdock. After that, I'd wash the roots and bundle them up. Then I'd go back to rooting up the burdock until evening came on and it grew dark. I worked so hard that there was hardly any time for sleeping. Many a sleepless night, I'd cry to myself, looking at my sleeping child's face, and wondering what would become of us in the future. The more I wondered whether I could manage, the more I'd cry. Night after night, I'd be in tears. Especially when the farmwork didn't go well, I'd get sad and start crying.

Compared to the terrible way that my husband died, I didn't have anything to cry about. I'd tell myself that if I didn't pull myself together, I couldn't bring up our child. Those ten years after the atom bomb were terribly hard. It was hell for those who died, but it was hell too even for those, like me, who were left alive.

In 1965, we lost our house and our land when they did the flood prevention work on the River Ōta. We were left with just 1 *tan* [¹/₄ acre] of dry land. The paddy fields too were taken for Kōyō's housing development. We got compensation, and with that we built a house and bought about 1 *tan* of land. I'm just a woman, so I couldn't buy very good land. It's a good kilometre away. Masae went to *kimono*-making school and got her certificate.

I thought that the money I got as compensation would soon disappear. And, anyway, it would have been miserable not to have had any land to farm. So that's why I made up my mind to buy some land. A widowed granny like me can't grow much in the way of crops, but it's nice, when you're getting on, to farm at your own pace, doing what you like best. The money I make goes on tax, or I give it to my daughter and grandchildren. I'm living with Masae and her husband now, so I'm happy. I think my husband must be happy too, as he lies under the turf.

9   Haruko Sumii

9 We Switched from Being Drapers to Farmers

Haruko Sumii

Death took away my first husband

I was born a long way from here. Nowadays it's called Toyohira in Yamagata District, but in the old days it used to be called Tsudani Village. I was born on 27 March 1912, so I'm 69 this year. It's true that I was born on 27 March, but if my parents had said I was born just four days later, I could have been an April child and been in a different year at school. But they were too honest to do that. Thanks to that, I started elementary school when I was 7. I wasn't a proper 8-year-old like the others, so I was really tiny. At school I was always in the front row.

My father was called Takajirō Kannauchi and he was in the first class to graduate from Hiroshima Teachers' Training College. It seems that in those days you could become a headmaster of an elementary school as soon as you graduated, so he became a headmaster in Yamaguchi District. I heard that, as our name Kannauchi [literally 'mine house'] tells us, in the past our family was involved in iron-ore mining. It's a family with a long history. My father's younger brother, Haruma, graduated from the Higher Mercantile Marine School in Tokyo. He was a captain on an occan-going shipping line. My family were land-owners, so you could say that we were part landlords and part farmers. We had quite a few tenants. Because my father was headmaster, it was my mother and grandfather who took charge of the farming. My father was hardly ever at home.

Living in our house, there were no fewer than eight of my father's brothers and sisters. It was a very large family. Since my father wasn't at home much, it was my mother who managed the house and the farm. She must have had a lot of worries. She fell ill and died when she was only 22. I was the elder daughter and I had one younger sister called Yachie. She's still fit and active.

In 1918, I entered Kobayashi Elementary School in Kobayashi,

77

Tsudani Village. From there, I went on to Kotodani Higher Elementary School. It was about 1¹/₂ *ri* [about 6 kilometres] from our house. On snowy days, I used to go there wearing straw boots that my Grandad had made for me. My feet often used to get chapped.

My mother died in 1915, and the following year my father was remarried, to a lady-teacher from Shimane Prefecture. After Higher Elementary School, I took the entrance examination for Ōshimo School (a private girls' school in Gion), even though my stepmother said to me:

'Knowing your school record, there's not much chance of you passing.'

I was only a child, but when I heard that, I thought to myself: 'Damn it!' There were two of us from Kotodani Higher Elementary School who took the exam and we both passed. I became a boarder. It was because my father was a headmaster that they let me go on with my studies. In those days, if people were just peasants, they didn't have the money to send their children to higher school.

I left Ōshimo School in 1928, when I was 17. Then I went to some relatives in Hiroshima, where they taught me sewing and good manners. After a year or so, I went to my uncle's in Tokyo. They didn't have any children, so they invited me to come and stay with them. It was about that time that they started to talk about finding me a husband and that's how I got to come here.

My husband was called Nagakazu Sumii and he had a good head on his shoulders. When we got married, I was 20 and my husband must have been 32, because there were twelve years between us. Being so clever, he'd come out top of his class at Sōtoku Middle School, and he'd even gone on to attend the Law Department at Meiji University. That was why he was so late getting married.

My father-in-law was called Tsunesaburō Sumii and he was the village headman in Kawauchi, but he died suddenly when my husband was in the third year of Law School. As a result, my husband had to give up his studies half-way. On top of that, my husband wasn't at all strong, suffering from *beri-beri* and other illnesses. So I suppose my mother-in-law thought it would be a good idea for Nagakazu to set up in business on his own. By a lucky coincidence, a draper by the name of Hayase in Koi Motomachi had decided to give up the business, so my mother-in-law bought it and set up as a draper.

The story gets a bit involved here, but my husband's elder brother was called Shigeki. My Auntie Kinuko from Toyohira married him. So I was already related to my husband's family before we got married. My husband, Nagakazu, was the second son, so he had to leave home. Since he wasn't very strong, they thought he'd do best being a draper or something like that. Brides don't exactly grow on trees, so me being my Auntie's niece, they thought I would do. Straight from Tokyo, I came here and got married. I was already 20 and people used to talk about '20-year-old grannies'. In those days, you were looked upon as an old person if you were over 20. So I jumped at the chance to get married. All the same, I suppose it's unusual for an aunt to marry an elder brother and her niece to marry the younger brother.

As soon as the wedding was over, we left for the draper's shop in Koi. We lived with my husband's mother and started business. At first, I didn't find it easy to treat the customers like a shopkeeper should. I didn't know anything about the drapery business, so I just did as my mother-in-law told me.

My daughter, Miwako, was born on 31 August 1932. It was still hot and I came to this house to have the baby, because it would have been inconvenient to have had the baby in the draper's shop . . . As it happened, my Auntie too had a baby boy in November. But in May of the following year, my Auntie was paralysed, so that she couldn't move half her body. She was still young – about 33, I should think.

As well as being the village headman, my father-in-law had inherited an indigo business, which had been in the family for generations. He had also been an agent for German dyes and sold them as far afield as Izumo (in Shimane Prefecture). It was my mother-in-law and my Auntie who had taken over the farmwork. My Auntie had had to put up with all sorts of stress and strain, so that's why she ended up with high blood pressure and collapsed at such an early age.

After that, things were chaotic. I had to bring up both my Auntie's baby and Miwako. My husband's illness also took a turn for the worse, so he couldn't look after the drapery business any more. Both here and at the draper's, things got too much to handle.

My Auntie lingered on for five years, but she eventually died on 8 December 1937. Then, when we were getting ready for the Buddhist ceremony to mark the 49th day after her death, my husband died. It was 16 January 1938. So we had one funeral after another. One blow followed another. I was still only 28. A human being has to be able to endure sorrow in order to live, but that doesn't make enduring the sorrow any easier.

Powdering up human bones

When my Auntie died, my brother-in-law, Shigeki, became a widower. Then I became a widow. Shigeki had two girls and two boys to look after. As for me, Miwako was still little (7 years old).

One night, my mother-in-law said to me:

'I'm sorry to ask you, but I wonder if you could take care of Shigeki's children.'

I had Miwako on my hands too . . . So I remarried, this time to Shigeki, in May 1942.

We left a relative of ours, called Hatsukichi Sumioka, to look after our land and we locked up the main house. Then we moved to the draper's shop in Koi and concentrated on running the business there. My second husband was on the small side, but he was fit and a hard worker. He was a very sensible and quiet type, but a good businessman. He used to go to Kyōto to buy our stock and the business did really well. They were happy times.

In 1943, I had our elder boy, Takanori, and in 1944, our younger boy, Yasuyuki. Then there were my Auntie's four children, so at one stage I was looking after seven children altogether. I brought them all up and that's why they all look after me now.

In January 1945, we gave up the draper's business, because people said that if we left our house here unoccupied, the army would confiscate it . . . In those days, if houses were left unoccupied, the army would come and take them over. We didn't want that to happen, so we gave up the draper's shop and came back here.

They said that if we didn't farm at least 3 *tan* [about ³/₄ acre] ourselves, the army would take over our land too. So we got Hatsukichi Sumioka to return 3 *tan* to us and we took up farming. Just over 1 *tan* was paddy fields, where we grew rice, while on the dry land we grew things like millet and potatoes. We switched from being drapers to farming, so it wasn't easy at all. At first, we didn't know how to go about it. Physically, it was hard for us too.

My husband liked tomatoes, so in the field in front of the house we planted a lot. Hard though the farmwork was, still we were happy.

On the morning of the 6th (the day of the atom bomb), my husband set off cheerfully with his lunch box, saying:

'Today's the last day of dismantling buildings, so I'll be back early . . .'

Never thinking what was going to happen, I saw him off and got on with looking after the children. Thinking that I'd go to the Agricultural Association (present-day Agricultural Cooperative) to get some rice polished, I'd just stepped out into the yard when there was an enormous BANG . . . Round the back of the house, two glass doors were left standing, as though somebody had removed them from their frames and stood them up. It must have been the blast wave from the atom bomb that did it. It was really strange that they didn't fall over. The ceiling of one room was pushed up and a shower of dust thrown down. We got round to repairing that ceiling just seven or eight years ago . . . When it happened, I couldn't believe my eyes.

I had to look after the children, so I stayed at home. Then somebody came to tell me that my Auntie's second boy, Shizuo, had got back as far as the shrine at Gion and that I should go there to collect him. I strapped the baby on my back and set off straightaway with the cart. But he wasn't there. There was no news either about what had become of my husband. The air-raid warning sounded again and again, so I dimmed the light, worrying all the time about Shizuo and my husband. Then, unexpectedly, Shizuo arrived back home.

'You've done well to get home, you've done well to get home!' I said to him and I was just about to put my arms round him when I noticed that half his body had been burnt black, including an arm and a leg. Shizuo was 13 then. He was in the first year of the Prefectural Commercial School and he told me that he'd been dismantling buildings at the foot of Hiji Hill. In those days, they had to give up their summer holidays. He was wearing a combat cap and short trousers. All the exposed parts of his body were burnt. He looked terrible. He told me that after the bomb exploded, he'd tried to run away from the flames, but he'd hardly known which way to turn, first going in one direction, then in another. He said that at the Prefectural Hospital in Ujina, they'd given him a rice ball to eat, but he'd felt sick and couldn't swallow it. He seemed to have gone off to the south, in the opposite direction to home. After that, he retraced his steps towards Hiroshima Station and eventually got home at 9 o'clock in the evening by following the railway line from the station.

By the morning of the 7th, he'd lost all energy and couldn't move much. He just kept on saying: 'It hurts; it hurts!' There was a first-aid station at Kawauchi Elementary School, so I put him on the cart and took him there to be looked at. I laid him down in the corridor and while we were waiting for treatment, the person next to us said:

'This boy's heart is beating violently. Isn't he dying?'
We waited for ages and then all they did was put a little talcum
powder on him. There wasn't any treatment they could give him.
Worrying all the time about my husband, I did everything I could to
look after Shizuo.

Somebody told me that powdered human bones were very effective,
and that gave me an idea. Down by the riverside, they were cremating
bodies day and night. So I thought that if I could collect some of
their bones . . . But I couldn't very well go and collect them myself.
So I asked the neighbours' children to pick up some bones and bring
them to me. I felt that I had to try anything that people said was
good . . .

I crushed the bones that they brought me in a stone mortar and
made them into powder. Then I picked away the scabs from the
burnt parts of Shizuo's body and sprinkled on the powder. If you
left the scabs on the burns, maggots soon got into them. So I stayed
by Shizuo all the time, picking off the scabs and sprinkling on the
powdered bone. Miwako, who was 13 then, looked after 1-year-old
Yasuyuki for me. I couldn't leave Shizuo's side and all he kept on
saying was: 'It hurts; it hurts!' I was with him constantly wiping away
the sweat and sprinkling on the powdered bone.

Shizuo really fought for his life. For about four months, he kept
on saying: 'The burns hurt; they hurt me!' But he also used to say, 'I
don't want to die', and he made a big effort to stay alive. Even after
six months, he still couldn't stand up. From about the end of
February, he'd say, 'I'm going to get up!' and he started to practise
walking. Holding on to the *shōji* screens, he'd go back and forth
across the room. He was a strong-willed boy.

He was off school for about one year. He had a keloid on his right
wrist, so he couldn't bend it. Although he went to Commercial
School, he couldn't use his abacus. About two years after he was
injured by the bomb, he had an operation at Imai Clinic in Midorii.
They took some tissue from his thigh and used it on his wrist. For a
long while, he was bald on that part of the back of his head which
hadn't been covered by the combat cap. I felt sorry for him, although
he didn't let on that it bothered him much . . . Nowadays, it's grown
back nicely, so that you wouldn't know what it was like. He's fit and
well now, and in 1960 he married Sachiko. He works for a dairy
company nearby. I'm living with them now. Although he's not my
own child, he looks after me well. I look upon him as my own son.

My husband appeared in my dreams

Now I'll tell you about my husband. Perhaps I didn't do all that I should have done for him. All my time went on looking after Shizuo . . . Some time after 10 August, I went one day to look for my husband. But although I searched for him, it was hopeless. I hadn't been able to search for him before, because I was still feeding the baby and I couldn't leave Shizuo. I made excuses to myself, because I could only search for him for one day. I'd heard that the Volunteer Corps had all been wiped out. Even the few who'd got back home had died one after another. So in my heart, I'd already given up my husband for lost.

On the one day I did go to look for him, I decided that it was hopeless and that he wouldn't come back. That night I went to sleep and had a dream that my husband was standing in the entrance porch. I could see him clearly, but he didn't say a word. Just as I was saying, 'You've come back . . .', I woke up. I wonder if he appeared in my dream because I hadn't searched enough for him? It made my heart bleed. I didn't know where he'd died or how he'd died. I was choked and, stifling my sobs, I wept to myself. I wondered what sort of heartbreaking thoughts had gone through my husband's mind as he died? How he must have missed his family and how he must have wanted to see his children! Even now I feel that it was wrong of me not to have found him.

During the next year or two, I had the same dream on four or five occasions. Each time, he didn't say a word. But I could clearly see him standing there in the entrance porch.

He'd left his false teeth behind, so they were all that we could put in his grave . . . There was nothing else. If he appeared in my dreams as much as that, it must have meant that his soul had come back to our house.

The eldest boy, Masaki (who was my Auntie's son and was 20 at that time) had been at the Wireless School in Nakano in Tokyo, so he wasn't here when the atom bomb was dropped. He told us that his school was shut down on 15 August and that was why he came home. When he got back and found that his younger brother, Shizuo, had been burnt black and that his father was missing, he couldn't hold back his tears. About 1948, he started a business in Hiroshima. It's a wholesale business, selling cottons. The fourth boy, Yasuyuki, works for Masaki.

For about a year, I couldn't face the farmwork. When I did get down to it, even though I wasn't much of a farmer, I had to grow enough to feed my children. So every day I could think of nothing else except scraping together enough food to feed them. Out of our 4 *tan* [about 1 acre], 1 *tan* 2 *se* [just over ¼ acre] was paddy fields and the rest was dry land. Until I got used to farming, it was really hard.

From the time when we'd had the draper's shop in Koi, I'd suffered from enteritis. Even in summer, I often had diarrhoea. People said that senna and cranesbill would do me good, so I tried taking them, but they didn't help. Even in summer, I'd tie a body warmer round my tummy and get on with the farmwork. What with the diarrhoea and the hard work, I got really thin. Still, I kept on with the farmwork, even though it certainly didn't do my illness any good. After they dropped the atom bomb, for about 15 years it was really hard, working as a woman on my own. I didn't have a penny in savings . . . Until Shizuo got married in 1960, I had a hard time of it.

Farming is really hard work. People say 'go hand-in-hand with the soil', but it's nothing like as easy as that. It seems to me that until you get used to it, there's nothing so trying and such hard work as farming. There's nothing easy about getting to the point where you can 'go hand-in-hand with the soil'. At long last, I've reached the point nowadays where, when I see the vegetables growing, I can feel some satisfaction and pleasure. It's a funny thing, but now that my days are numbered, I've come to see the good side of farming. We inherited the land as property from our ancestors and, thanks to that, we could survive. We had the land which our ancestors had passed on to us and that was how I could bring up the children and give them an education. (The third and fourth boys both graduated from university.)

They say that what happens to you in this life is already decided by your previous existence. I haven't got much life left, but I've decided to look after my health and do the best I can. But you never know when misfortune is going to strike. On 28 October 1973, I'd come out of Aki Yaguchi Station (on the Geibi line) and was hurrying home across Asa Bridge, when I was hit by a car driven by a young man. I was thrown up on to the car bonnet and then hurled on to the river embankment. I hit my head and my hips and had to take things easy for two months. My hips were terribly bruised and I've ended up bent over like this. People never know what life has in store for them. Because of what happened, I don't suppose I'll live as long as I might have done. All the same, I'm living out my last days, thankful for every new day that's granted to me.

10   Ochika Matsuda

10 The War Turned My Life Upside Down

Ochika Matsuda

My husband and daughter went off with the Volunteer Corps

This year I've reached the age when I'll get an invitation to the reception for old people put on by the town. I was born on 28 May 1901, so I'll be just turned 80. I'm hoping to still be alive on Respect for the Aged Day on 15 September, so that I can go to the reception.

The place where I was born was Jōrakuji, in Yagi Village, in Asa District (present-day Yagi in Satō). As well as being peasants, we made clogs out of Paulownia wood. After I'd finished elementary school in Yagi, I spent my time sewing and looking after the babies. I got married in October 1921. My husband was called Tomezō Matsuda. He was tall and thin. He had no less than ten brothers and sisters, and he was the fourth boy. I heard that his parents had so many children that when they had Tomezō, they gave him that name [literally 'Stop Producing'] because they thought it was best not to have any more. My husband was a good-hearted person. He hardly scolded me. We had a big farm, with 1 *tan* [about ¼ acre] of paddy fields and as much as 1 *chō* 2 *tan* [about 3 acres] of dry land.

We produced a lot of hemp and silkworms. Everywhere in the house, we had trays of silkworms. I remember once one of the kids went missing and I looked all over for him. Would you believe it, I found him sleeping under one of the silkworm shelves! What a relief!

Sometimes my mother-in-law used to make millet dumplings, coated with bean jam. In those days, the food we ate was pretty poor. Tomezō was a really hard worker. As you can see, I'm the type who does things slowly. He often used to say to me:

'Hurry up and get out in the fields!'

Early on the morning of the 6th (the day of the atom bomb), while I was cooking the rice, my husband made some straw sandals to wear. Our second girl, Toshie, was also due to go off with the Volunteer Corps and he made some straw sandals for her too. Toshie had been a teacher at Iwakuni Elementary School (in Iwakuni,

Yamaguchi Prefecture) but, because she was worried about air raids, she'd resigned and was helping out on the farm. That was how she came to go off with her father in the Volunteer Corps.

I had eight children. Our eldest boy, Hitoshi, was 19. Our second boy, Isamu, was in the fifth year of elementary school. Our third boy, Tadashi, was in the third year of elementary school. Our fourth boy, Susumu, was 80 days old. Our eldest girl, Masae, was a teacher at Gion Elementary School. Our second girl was Toshie, whom I mentioned before. Our third girl was Yayoi and our fourth girl was Hisako. We raised a lot of children, didn't we? Well, instead of us raising them, I suppose you could say that they raised themselves.

Later that morning, I thought I would sieve the threshed barley and I went to borrow a sieve from Mrs Tatsumoto next door. Just as I got back home, there was a blinding flash. At that time, our house was being rebuilt. The old house had been washed away in the great flood of 1943 (20 September) . . . When the River Furu's embankment was breached, as many as twelve houses were washed away in Shimo Nukui. Due to that, we had been living in the barn. Because the walls still hadn't been put up in the new house, it wasn't damaged by the blast wave from the atom bomb.

After the blinding flash, I looked over towards Hiroshima and a great mass of smoke rose up. It never crossed my mind that my husband and the others might have been hurt. I just stood there, looking and wondering what had happened. Later on, we all met at Mrs (Tamano) Momoki's and made rice balls for the people who'd gone with the Volunteer Corps and were due back in the evening. But no one came back, including my husband. They'd been hit by the atom bomb, so how could they come back?

It's doubtful that they were the remains of my daughter

As evening gave way to night, we gradually realised that Hiroshima had been totally destroyed and that everybody who'd gone off with the Volunteer Corps was done for. On the morning of the 7th, I heard that the survivors had been brought to the Yutani Factory or Shōsō Temple in Gion. Straightaway, I set off to look for my husband and daughter.

Inside the Yutani Factory, there were a lot of injured people. They were so terribly burned that when I walked around, looking at them, you couldn't tell who was who. Their bodies were charred all over and their faces had swollen up. I can't tell you how terrible they

looked. It was heartbreaking to hear them saying: 'Give me some
water; give me some water!' As I went back and forth among the
wounded, looking for my husband, I could only hope that he wouldn't
be among them.

I couldn't find him there, so I thought I'd go to Shōsō Temple.
Just as I was about to leave the factory, Yayoi arrived. She was
panting, and said:

'Mum, come back quickly! Dad's come back . . .'

'Is he all right?'

'I don't think he's breathing . . .'

I flew back home. I think it was about 2 o'clock on the afternoon
of the 7th.

I heard that my husband had been found dead in the River
Motoyasu. Mr Masuda from Nakachōshi found him and brought him
back by boat. Just like Yayoi had said, he wasn't breathing at all.
How could he have been?

Hitoshi had been called away to do guard duty in Misasa. But he'd
been worried about the family, so he'd got permission to visit home
until 4 o'clock. It was Hitoshi who'd taken the cart to collect his
father's body from Takase, where it had been brought back by boat.

They'd laid my husband out on the bare boards of one of the
rooms in the barn. He was naked and didn't even have anything on
his feet. His whole body was burned terribly. His skin was hanging
off him in shreds. His peeled skin lay in a pile at his feet. You could
hardly bear to look at his charred and swollen face. It was so awful,
it broke my heart. You couldn't imagine it was the same person
who'd gone off, saying: 'I'll be back early today . . .'

When we moved his body, his tummy rumbled and dark-coloured
blood flowed out of his mouth . . . It was an indescribably awful way
to die.

We held the wake in the dim light of the barn. The light was dim
because of the black-out. We didn't even have a coffin, but we
dressed him in a fresh silk *kimono*. About 11 o'clock on the morning
of the 8th, we lined up on the riverside the bodies of my husband
and our neighbours Ayako Ishibashi, Kenichi Tatsumoto and Tadaichi
Nakada. Then we cremated them.

Toshie had been on my mind all the time too. On the 7th, our
neighbour Tōsaku Itao came to tell me:

'I brought her back by boat as far as Ōshiba.'

I heard that, in the boat, she just kept on calling for me: 'Mum,
Mum!' Mr Itao said:

'I thought she was really suffering, so I left her at Ōshiba.'

Straightaway, I ran to Ōshiba, but I couldn't find her. It was then that I turned back to the Yutani Factory, which I told you about before. Toshie's story and my husband's are getting tangled up, so you might not be able to follow what I'm saying . . . Anyhow, neither my husband nor Toshie were at Yutani. They'd said that my daughter was still breathing when she was in the boat. But where could she have been taken to now? I was at a loss to know what to do.

It was just gone noon on the 8th, when word came from Ōshiba:

'We've just started to cremate your daughter now. Please come tomorrow morning to collect her bones.'

I sent Masae to go and collect Toshie's remains, because I was in the middle of cremating my husband. In fact, nobody knows whose are the bones which Masae brought back with her. Even now, I'm doubtful that they really were Toshie's. Still, I didn't see what else we could do, so we put the bones into the grave, together with my husband's.

What with having a baby at my breast and growing children in the house, it was really hard after that. For the first ten years after the war, life was so hard, day after day, that I even wished I could die and go to join my husband and Toshie. I can't tell you how hard it was.

Hitoshi put his back into the farmwork. In 1956 he started processing pickles made from Hiroshima greens. The business has grown and now he's doing well. The war turned my life upside down, but I'm grateful to say that I'm living in peace now.

11   Yae Kirido

11 I'm an Atom-Bomb Widow

Yae Kirido

The water in the paddy field flashed

I was born on 28 February 1910. I'll be 71 this year. The place where I was born was called Onji, in Naka Fukawa, in Kōyō. We grew only rice there. I had two elder brothers and a younger sister, so I was the elder daughter. After leaving elementary school, I took lessons in *kimono*-making.

I came here to get married on 27 May 1931. My husband was called Masato and I should think he was 29. When they dropped the atom bomb, he was 44. On the farm, we had 3 *tan* [about ³/₄ acre] of paddy fields and 2 *tan* [about ¹/₂ acre] of dry land. In the old days, they used to talk about '5 *tan* peasants', and that's what we were. We raised silkworms, grew hemp, and such like. We used to peel the hemp at a communal steamer round the back of the Hachiman Shrine. We grew a lot of barley and millet. Some families were so poor that they even ate millet gruel. Even though it wasn't much, we grew some rice, so luckily we didn't have to eat millet gruel.

My husband didn't drink or smoke. Instead, he loved sweet things. He often used to eat sugar like sweets. My grandson, Kiyoshi, is 22 now and, just like my husband, he doesn't drink or smoke either. It must be in the blood.

He wasn't the grumbling type. I was never once scolded by him. Since my childhood days in Fukawa, I'd always been working so I didn't find the work here that hard. I was famous for getting up early in summer. In July and August, it's a good idea to work in the cool of the morning. I'd already have done a good bit of work by breakfast-time.

On the morning of 6 August too, I got up at 4 o'clock. My husband was going off with the Volunteer Corps, so I packed up his dinner and gave him his breakfast. Then, straightaway, I went out into the fields. I didn't see him off or say 'Bye-bye, Darling', like the office

93

workers' wives say to their husbands. While I was weeding the paddy field near the shrine, the villagers were making a racket as the Volunteer Corps set off. Among them was my husband, but although I thought to myself that the Volunteer Corps must be setting off, I just kept on weeding the paddy field.

When it happened, the water in the paddy field flashed like lightning and I felt as though my back was scorched. It was so hot that, without thinking, I put my hand on my back. Even now, I can't forget how hot my back felt at that moment. I was startled, so, straightening up, I looked at the sky. It was pitch dark. Our neighbour, Mitsujirō Masuda, came to the shrine too. Looking at the sky over towards Hiroshima, he kept on saying:

'I wonder what's happened?'

Not knowing what it was, we just stood there looking at the sky in amazement.

About 5 o'clock on the 6th, somebody said to me:

'The injured members of the Volunteer Corps have got back to Kanda Bridge in Furuichi, so please go to them.'

I can't remember who it was who came and told me.

I spread some straw matting on the cart and, taking a pillow with me, set off. Keiroku Fujimoto, from next door, went with me, because his wife (Haruko) too had gone off with the Volunteer Corps. On the way, we came across a lot of injured people. There was a stream of people running away from Hiroshima and some of them had the skin hanging off their hands.

My husband hadn't got back to Furuichi. There was nothing for it but to return home, pulling an empty cart. Haruko from next door ended up as a missing person too.

Inside the house, the blast wave had made a terrible mess of things. That night I couldn't get a wink of sleep. My husband hadn't got back and there was no news of him either.

On the morning of the 7th, I left home about 5 o'clock and set off for Hiroshima to look for him. Our elder girl, Yoshie, was 10 and our younger girl, Hiroko, was 2, so I left them with the neighbours. I hurried as far as Aioi Bridge (the epicentre of the atomic explosion), following the river embankment from Nishihara. In the bamboo thickets alongside the river embankment there were many burnt and injured people, some of them lying down, some sitting up, but all of them groaning. After crossing Misasa Bridge, I went on to Aioi Bridge. Inside the town there were many people and horses lying about dead. The people were mostly men. Here and there, in among the dead, there were some people who were still alive. They were begging for water.

I went as far as Jisen Temple at the side of Aioi Bridge. Beyond that, the fires were still burning, so they wouldn't let me go any further. I walked through the town all day, but I couldn't find my husband.

Bringing up two children

I went out to search for my husband on the 8th too, but I couldn't find any corpse that looked like his. Seeing how badly Hiroshima had been burnt, it seemed to me that, however much I searched, I'd never find him, so I went back home. That night too, my husband didn't come back. I fell asleep, thinking that there was less and less chance that he'd return. A third day passed, and then a fourth, but still he didn't come back. I didn't know where he was or what had become of him.

However much I liked farmwork, for a while I didn't feel like working at all. Anyway, I suppose that if anyone had gone to work in the fields at that time, people would have laughed at them.

After about a month of thinking about my husband and not doing any work, the fields were full of weeds. A lot of the cucumber plants had shrivelled up. Even those that weren't already dead hadn't been propped up, so they ended up growing flat along the ground. The baby was 2 years old. Strapping it on my back, or holding it in my arm, I got down to work. From that day on, I worked for the kids' sake. I thought that I had to bring the kids up until they could stand on their own two feet.

Collecting nightsoil was really hard. I used to go as far as Danbara (a district that was relatively lightly damaged because it was sheltered by Hiji Hill) to collect nightsoil with Mr Fujimoto from next door. Two or three times a month, I'd load up 3 tubs on the cart and go to collect nightsoil. I used to get up at 2 or 3 o'clock in the morning.

My neighbour, Tadaichi Miyamoto, said to me:

'A long time ago, when I'd been injured and was in hospital, your old man let me have some nightsoil. I must pay you back.'

So he gave me some nightsoil on two or three occasions and repaid me in that way. I was really grateful. Even now, I haven't forgotten it. Because my husband did him a favour, he helped me. That's the way the world is. If you help other people, they'll help you in return. But you know, I've lived all this time without relying on anybody.

People don't help. No one gives you even a single penny for nothing. Anyway, what I've done is to spend my money on my children. I sent them both to high school. Then I let Yoshie take lessons in *kimono*-making for two years and lessons in knitting for one year. I let Hiroko learn dress-making too. I'm proud of what I did. Yoshie's got a hard-working husband and Hiroko is happy, living over towards Chiba.

My daughter, Yoshie, takes in sewing. I'm living with her and her husband, and since she's my own flesh and blood, I don't have to stand on ceremony. I haven't a white hair on my head. I'm living happily now.

I was widowed by the atom bomb when I was 35. My kids were still small and there was the farmwork to be done, so it's been a long, hard struggle up till now. What with the kids and the farming, I never had the time to think about men. All the hardship, and all the work, I had to face just on my own. Since she's a woman, Yoshie understands what a hard time I had and looks after me well. It's a good thing that she was a girl.

Nowadays, I've got about 1 *tan* 3 *se* [about ⅓ acre] under vegetables. You won't find a single weed in my field. I still don't dawdle around, so I manage to grow pretty good vegetables, although an old, widowed granny like me can't be expected to grow a lot.

I keep pretty good health. There's just one thing that might make you laugh if I tell you, but some fried oysters disagreed with me once. I had a tummy ache and didn't know what to do with myself. So I had to lie down. That's the only time I've been ill enough to lie down. But because of my age, my legs ache a bit nowadays.

My husband built our family grave in September 1937. It's his parents who are buried in it, but ten years ago one of my relatives persuaded me to have my husband's Buddhist name engraved on it. We never got back his body or anything of his, so there wasn't anything to put in the grave. We just put in the piece of paper that had his Buddhist name written on it. Ten years ago, we had his Buddhist name engraved on it, so at long last he's resting in a grave.

Even now, I often dream about my husband. I get up early in the morning and get on with my work. Because I work myself into the ground, you might think that I'd be too tired to have dreams. But I often do dream even now, although it's only about my husband.

12   Sada Tatsumoto

12 I Went to an Island to Look for My Husband

Sada Tatsumoto

We planned to build a house

The place I was born used to be called Nakasuji, in Mikawa Village, in Takamiya District (now it's called Yasufuruichi). I was born there on 21 October 1894. I'll be 87 this year. I'm a bit deaf, but otherwise I'm fit and still doing the farmwork. My father was called Ishita Nekoshima and my mother was called Oseki.

There were five of us kids, but only two of us – me and my younger brother, Asaichi (now 85 years old) – lived to grow up. We grew barley and Kyō greens on the farm. My mother was often ill and she died young, when I was 12. I used to help my father. From an early age, I'd do things like looking after the babies and helping with the farmwork . . . I hardly knew what it was to play. I was a hard worker and the villagers used to say that I was a good girl to my father.

When I was 22, I came here (Kawauchi in Satō) to get married. My husband was called Toyoji and he was four years older than me. My husband wasn't the eldest son, so we didn't have much land. I'll tell you what we used to do to make a living. At night, we used to twist hemp into thread. So we'd work hard in the fields during the day and then, when night came on, we'd twist the hemp. Another time, we raised silkworms. We raised so many that we had to build a barn for them. My word, we were busy! I worked as hard as any man. I had to, because if I hadn't worked like that, there wouldn't have been anything to eat.

What with my mother dying early, I had a hard time when I was young. Then, after I got married, life was hard again, struggling to feed us all. We were tenant farmers, and we were so poor that we had to be careful not to waste a single thing. We just had the farm to make a living from, so we had to work like mad. Take a look at my shoulders. The right one's higher than the left, isn't it? That's because I used my right arm so much. My husband was a hard worker too.

99

I had seven kids. When they dropped the atom bomb, our eldest boy, Yoshihiro, was a soldier in Central China. Our second boy, Mitsuaki, was 18 and he was helping us on the farm. Our third boy, Hiromi, was in the second year of elementary school. Our eldest girl was already married. Our second girl, Tomie, was killed by the atom bomb when she was 28. She was still single and was helping us on the farm. That's why she went off with the Volunteer Corps and was killed. We'd wanted her to get married, but all the young men had been called up into the army, so we couldn't find anyone for her. Our third girl, Mitsue, was working at the Mitsubishi Heavy Industry factory in Gion. Our fourth girl, Shizuko, was in the sixth year of elementary school.

People like us had really bad luck. In the flood of 1943, our main house was washed away and the storehouse tumbled over. We got our ration of timber and, although there was only enough for a little house, we were planning to go ahead and build it. On the morning of the day when they dropped the atom bomb, my husband said to me as he set off:

'This work (dismantling buildings) will finish today, so from tomorrow let's get ready to build the house.'

I was pleased when I heard that. Since the flood, we'd been living in a shack.

That morning, I was working in the field, tying up the cucumber plants. When I felt the flash from the atom bomb, my hand jerked up to my forehead. There was a tremendous BANG and when I looked over towards Hiroshima, there was a mass of reddish-black smoke, looking a bit like a thunder cloud. The smoke kept on rising endlessly, as though it was never going to stop . . . You just can't describe what that smoke was like. I can see it even now . . .

My husband had said that he'd bring back the wood for building a Community Hall. On the morning of the 6th, he'd loaded up some vegetables to take to market and as soon as the air-raid siren sounded the all-clear, he'd set off, while it was still dark. Being deputy-leader of the Volunteer Corps and head of the Neighbourhood Association, he was a busy person. He often used to take our second son, Mitsuaki, with him when he went to collect nightsoil and that morning, too, he'd set off with Mitsuaki. About 6 o'clock in the morning, Mitsuaki and his father had gone their separate ways in the centre of Hiroshima. Mitsuaki had set off home with a load of timber from the dismantled buildings.

Our daughter, Tomie, had gone off with Mr Tomimura from next door, taking with her a lunch box for her father. People had said to her:

'Since your father has turned out, you don't have to go . . .'

But she went anyway, saying:

'I want to join the Volunteer Corps and go to Hiroshima. I don't mind being killed by a bullet. It's all for our country . . .'

On the day before she died, she'd been spreading nightsoil on the paddy field for us. She worked so hard in the fields, you'd have thought it was her own farm. She had a good head on her shoulders. She didn't have such a pretty face, but her health was good and she was a good girl. The best one always dies first. That's the way it is. She went off taking her father's lunch box with her, but whether she handed it over to him or not . . .

Mitsuaki told me that when the atom bomb exploded, he'd already got back as far as that shrine in Misasa where people go to get rid of their warts. He was leading the horse and cart. He told me that as soon as he felt the blinding flash, there was an enormous BANG, and for a moment he couldn't see a thing. The horse was terrified too. Its legs went weak and it just seemed dazed. In places where sliding doors and shutters had crashed down on to the road, the cart made a tremendous clatter as Mitsuaki made his way home. It was about 9 o'clock in the morning when he got back.

It said on the village loudspeaker that 'The Volunteer Corps has been wiped out.' Mitsuaki said, 'We must go and look for them', and he set off in the afternoon. He got back as evening came on and told us that the town was a sea of fire and that he hadn't been able to get near the place where they'd been dismantling the houses. Since about noon, a stream of injured people had been fleeing from Hiroshima. When you looked at them, they had hardly any clothes on their bodies, even underwear. The ones who were terribly burned had skin hanging off them and were walking along like ghosts, with their hands stretched out in front of them. I realised something awful had happened. Neither my husband nor Tomie had come back. I was thinking to myself that perhaps they'd stopped off at somebody's house and were being looked after there, or that they might come back unexpectedly at any time. That night, sitting in our house, which had had its ceiling pushed up, I waited till dawn broke.

They died like cats and dogs

My husband often used to say:

'You never know when I might get caught in an air raid. I might be lying around dead, like some cat or dog . . .'

On the next day, I set off with Mitsuaki to search for my husband and Tomie. There were a lot of bodies lying around dead by the roadside. It made me think that perhaps my husband really had died like some cat or dog, as he was always saying. I had no idea what had become of my husband or Tomie. Perhaps they'd already been taken away and cremated, or perhaps their bodies had sunk in the river? There was no trace of either of them . . .

After five days or so, I took the boat on my own to Nino Island (in Hiroshima Bay). I'd heard that many bodies had been picked up there . . . I walked all over the island, searching. Shacks had sprung up and many orphaned children had been brought there. On the beaches, people were cremating and burying the bodies which had been carried there by the current. I didn't have anything to go on, so it was just a shot in the dark. I think I must have been the only one from here (Kawauchi in Satō) who went as far as Nino Island to search.

It must have been about the 15th that a neighbour came to tell me:

'A body's been found by Yoshijima Prison that's a lot like your old man.'

Straightaway, I went there to take a look, but it was someone different. He was built a lot like my husband, but . . . He'd died leaning against the prison wall. He was wearing a jacket like a *happi*, with a towel tied round his head like a scarf, and was sitting with his head drooping forward. His body was rotting and he'd got maggots coming out of his nose. The poor man was decomposing. I can see him now! After that, I gave up searching for my husband and Tomie. Mitsuaki went into Hiroshima several times to look for people from the village, and perhaps because of that, after a while he got a sore throat and was under the doctor for about a month. And do you know, if he cut himself, it generally festered . . . But I seemed to be all right.

In the end, we never found out what happened to either my husband or Tomie. All we could do was put their photographs into the grave . . . Neither my husband nor my daughter came to me in my dreams. I had to get on with the farmwork. I couldn't go on grieving for ever. I didn't have time for weeping. They were all growing children, right down to Hiromi in the second year of elementary school. In the past, my husband and I had worked really hard to get our 8 *tan* [about 2 acres] of land. Now I had to work like a donkey to farm it. I had a hard time until the kids could stand on their own two feet. I thought to myself that I must bring them up to be good children who wouldn't show me up. I thought that even if I had to become a rickshaw-puller to do it, I'd put them through school.

Mitsuaki worked hard on the farm. Even when his pals went off to have a good time, he never went with them. All his time went into helping me on the farm. He used to collect nightsoil for me. I let both Shizuko and Hiromi stay on at high school. Shizuko even went to Ōsaka Pharmaceutical College. They all grew up to be good kids and I never had to worry about what they were up to.

I love farming. Already when I was as little as 6 or 7, I got into the habit of working, and even now my body won't let me stay still. After Mitsuaki got married, things got a lot easier, but up till then, we were always as poor as church mice, and it was work, work all day long. It's a funny thing, but I still get uneasy if I see any weeds growing, even in somebody else's fields. So much so that I start to wonder whether I ought to secretly do the weeding for them. My daughter-in-law says to me:

'You've put your children through school and worked your whole life, so why don't you take it easy now, without working?'

But it upsets me to see weeds growing in a field, so I can't stop myself doing it.

I grow all the vegetables that we eat in the house. I grow them even though my daughter-in-law tells me not to. I grow my favourite vegetables, and if we've got too many, I give them away. On my own land, I can grow the crops that I like best. They say to me:

'Please stop. If you grow too many vegetables, we won't know what to do with them all. So don't grow any more!'

But I enjoy tending my vegetable field.

I'm getting on now, so I can't work that hard, but I can still do the odd jobs, like weeding the fields. We grow as much as 4 *tan* [about 1 acre] of Hiroshima greens and when it comes to thinning them out, I'm as good as the next man. When I was little, I got nothing worse than dysentery, and I've never been seriously ill. I'm just a bit hard of hearing, and I get a bit of toothache too.

As for money, I leave that to my daughter-in-law. You can't take money with you when you die . . . As long as I've got enough for my needs, I'm happy. They all look after me, so I've got nothing to grumble about.

When my eldest boy, Yoshihiro, came back after the war, he said: 'Even on the battlefield, I never saw anything as terrible as what the atom bomb did.'

Unless you've experienced it, you can't really understand the horror of the atom bomb. I've told my grandchildren about it again and again, but they don't take it seriously. I'm an old woman now and I haven't got much longer to live, but I could die with an easy mind if only people could understand how terrible the atom bomb is.

13   Shizuko Ryōso

13 An Invalid Like Me Was Left Alive

Shizuko Ryōso

'You're pretending to be ill'

I was born on 6 September 1899. I'll be 82 this year. It was a place called Nagasako, in Ōbayashi Village, in Asa District (present-day Kabe). My family had been peasants for generations. There were four of us kids. I had an elder brother and then two younger brothers and two younger sisters. Oh! Wait a minute, that makes six altogether!

After leaving Ōbayashi Elementary School, I helped on the farm. We had a good 1 *chō* [about 2¹/₂ acres] of land, so we were kept busy. Since my childhood days, I'd been scything the grass and collecting firewood, so I could do them with my eyes closed. I used to thresh the rice too.

I came here on 6 December 1916. I was 17 and it was an arranged marriage. There was I, working in the fields, and I didn't even know that arrangements were going ahead for my marriage. I was only 17, so I didn't know what marriage was all about. My mother died on 12 October, when she was 38. As soon as the 49-day mourning period was over, I got married. My husband was called Kameshirō Ryōso. He was born in 1890, so he was 8 or 9 years older than me.

From Nagasako to Midorii, I travelled on a cart lit up with paper lanterns. Then from Midorii, I came to this house on foot, together with the people who were carrying my bridal furniture. I was wearing a white bridal *kimono*. My husband was a wonderful man. He was honest and sensible and there was nothing crafty about him. I'm not saying he was a superior sort of person; it's more that he was warm-hearted . . . After coming here, I never once felt disappointed in him.

We had 2 *tan* [about ¹/₂ acre] of paddy fields and 2 *tan* of dry land, so we grew rice and vegetables. Even though we grew rice, we didn't eat white rice. In those days, we used to eat rice mixed with barley, together with pickled vegetables. We grew a lot of millet, Kyō greens and cucumbers. My husband used to go regularly to Hiroshima with his horse and cart to collect nightsoil.

I wasn't well on 6 August. Since I was young, I'd often been laid low with rheumatism. There were times when I couldn't get up, even to do a simple thing like cook the rice. Sometimes my husband even asked me: 'Are you pretending to be ill?' There was nothing to show I was ill, but my arms and legs ached so much, I didn't know what to do with myself.

That morning too, I couldn't get up, so I was still lying on the mattress. I heard my husband's voice coming from the neighbour's yard. He was saying:

'Today's the last day, so let's be off . . .'

Those words were the last that I heard my husband say in this life.

My elder boy was called Isao and my younger boy Tsukasa. My elder girl, Toshie, had died young, when she was only 4; and my younger girl, Fujie, had died just after her first birthday. So all I was left with were my two boys.

Isao had been called up by the army in 1941 and was somewhere in Central China. He came back in June 1946. I'll never forget the day he got back. I was working in the fields when somebody called, 'Mum!' There he was standing on the embankment with a big rucksack on his back . . . It was like seeing the sun rising from that spot. I was so happy! Looking back on it now, it was the happiest moment in the 80 years that I've lived. Ever since then, he's stayed with me and farmed the land. I'm grateful to him for that.

Oh dear! I'm sorry about that. I started off talking about the atom bomb, and here I am telling you about my boy coming back from the war. It made me so happy that I've gone and told you about it first . . .

When it happened, there was an enormous bang. The nearest you can get to it would be a noise like 'DOKAN'. A black cloud rose up in the sky to the south. Doors and *shōji* screens were sent flying, and the ceiling was pushed up. I was in the house at the time and I was really shaken . . . It left me dazed. I went outside and just stood there, looking at the sky, and asking myself what on earth could have happened.

After a while, somebody from Kami Nukui came by, saying:

'The Kawauchi Volunteer Corps has been wiped out.'

About evening time, people were saying:

'The survivors will come back by boat to Takase Jetty.'

I couldn't get up, so I got our younger boy, Tsukasa, who was 16 by then, to run down there for me. But my husband wasn't among them.

Even when night came, my husband didn't come back. Since I was ill, I just couldn't go to Hiroshima to search for him. So from the next day onwards, I'd pack up a lunch box for Tsukasa and send him off with the neighbours to look for his father.

When Tsukasa got back, he told me:

'There are dead bodies everywhere on the roads. A lot of schoolgirls were dead, with their heads dipping into the fire brigade's water tanks.'

Two or three days later, he said:

'It's dreadful. The dead bodies, and the injured people who are still alive, are crawling with maggots.'

I suppose he must have gone out searching for about four or five days. I can't remember exactly now. When night came on, I'd get the feeling that my husband might come back at any time, so hour after hour I'd sit up without sleep. But we didn't even get his dead body back. One day just followed another, without us being able to arrange a funeral. Another thing was that nobody came to say they were sorry, because all the neighbours had been hit by misfortune too . . .

No body and no remains

It was a long while before I'd admit that my husband wouldn't come back and that he must be dead. In fact, the feeling that he's still alive will probably be with me until I die. Many a night, I couldn't sleep. I'd often dream about him too. Even now, I still see him sometimes in my dreams. He's supposed to be dead, but because I've never seen his body, I don't think I'll ever lose the feeling that he's still alive somewhere in Hiroshima. That thought's always been with me for these past 36 years.

We didn't have anything to put into his grave. There was nothing special that he'd left behind, so we didn't put anything in the grave. He had worked hard because he believed it was for the sake of the country, but then the atom bomb murdered him. Words can't express how I feel. I used to think all sorts of things, but it's all in the past now, and there's no point in brooding on it.

After the autumn breeze set in, Tsukasa and I got down to the farmwork. I couldn't afford to let the rheumatism keep me on my mattress. I wasn't running a temperature and if I hadn't made an effort, the fields would have ended up a mass of weeds and we wouldn't have been able to eat. Tsukasa stayed with me and helped until Isao came back from the war. In fact, now that all these years have passed, I can tell you that, because he was 16, Tsukasa too ought to have gone with the Volunteer Corps on that day. It was because I was ill that he asked the office and they let him off. What else can you say, except that he was really lucky?

I used to send him off with the neighbours to collect nightsoil. I'd wake him up at 2 o'clock in the morning. I could tell that he hated collecting the nightsoil, but still he did what I asked him. When I had trouble with my walking, he'd put me on the bicycle cart and take me to the massager's.

In every house in the village, somebody had died, so we couldn't help out each other with the work. There was nothing for it but for Tsukasa and me to soldier on together. Because I was ill, sometimes my husband's younger brother or my younger brother's wife (who lived in Mitaka, in Okimi) came to help me. That was a big help.

What gave me strength was that all the women in the village had been widowed by the atom bomb at the same time. My elder brother often used to comfort me when I was depressed. He'd say: 'You've got to realise that you're not the only one who's become a widow.'

As I already told you, my elder boy, Isao, came back in June 1946. After that, things eventually got easier. The two boys would go together to collect nightsoil and that made a big difference to growing vegetables in the fields. They used to take the iron-wheeled handcart as far as Midori to collect nightsoil. They had to go as far as Ujina and Midori, because all the houses nearer had been destroyed. After about a year, they switched to a horse and cart. That way, they could collect much more nightsoil for spreading on the fields, and the crops really improved.

Tsukasa soon started to work for a Rubber Company. Isao married Toshie in the autumn of 1946, and he kept on working on the farm. But after a time, he started to work for the Kawauchi Village Agricultural Cooperative and Asa Water Enterprise Group. So Toshie took up 'housewife farming', and I helped her as a 'granny farmer'. My rheumatism got easier. Nowadays, I do jobs like weeding the fields and preparing the meals. Toshie works at the Agricultural Cooperative's Nursery now, so Isao (who retired two years ago) and me are in charge of the farm these days.

My eldest grandchild is grown up now. In fact, he's 32. I've got four grandchildren in all, two of Isao's and two of Tsukasa's. I'm really grateful that the last years of my life have passed happily.

All the same, I still dream about my husband sometimes. Even though it's such a long time ago now since my husband and I were together, in my dreams it seems just like yesterday. After getting married, when I was 17, there was one hardship after another, what with my illness and the atom bomb and the rest of it. I'm really grateful that I've managed to live on till now.

Whether it's due to something bad that I did in a previous life, or to some terrible karma, I don't know. But whatever else happens, I don't want there to be another war. All I know is that we mustn't let our children and grandchildren go through that hell. Make sure you don't miss that out when you're writing it down!

14   Kinuyo Tade

14 With an Unweaned Baby Strapped on My Back

Kinuyo Tade

My whole family went to Hawaii

If my baby had been three years old, I'd have had to turn out with the Volunteer Corps as well. But Hideaki (the third son) was still 2. If he'd been just a year older, I'd have gone with the Volunteer Corps like my husband and I'd have been killed too. I still think that it was my baby who saved me. It's thanks to him that I'm alive today and talking to you now. There shouldn't be any wars. It was terrible. I think there should never be another war.

I'll start from when I was born. You're the first person to ask me to go back that far.

I was born in Nagatsuka, in Gion, in Asa District. Let me see, it must have been 25 January 1907. I'll tell you about my brothers and sisters. The eldest girl – my elder sister, you understand – was called Isao. Next was the second girl – me. My younger sister was called Shizue. Next came my young brothers; the elder one was called Itaru and the younger one Masuo. Except for me, the others all went to Hawaii. For some reason, I was the only one who didn't go.

My father was called Masutarō and he had fought in the Russo-Japanese War. After coming back from the war, he went over to Hawaii. At that time, I was still in my mother's tummy. After I'd been born, I suppose my father must have sent for my mother. Because I was so tiny, my mother left me behind and went off to join my father. So I was brought up by my Granny and Grandad.

I was the only one out of the five children who didn't have much to do with my parents. I must have been born under an unlucky star.

When I was small, I really wanted to go to Hawaii, where my parents were. I wrote I don't know how many letters, asking them to send for me. Sometimes I'd ask people who'd come back to Japan from Hawaii on a visit to take back a letter for me. Just once before the war they came back to Japan and I saw my parents then. My father died in an air raid on Hawaii during the Pacific War. My mother died in Hawaii too, when she was 90. I've thought that I'd like to go and see their grave, but when you get to my age (74), there's not much more you can do than think about it.

After the war was over, I thought I could go to Hawaii, but it turned out that they weren't allowed to send for me. And, of course, my husband (Eijirō) had been killed by the atom bomb. It must have been fate from a previous life. I'm an unlucky person. My whole life's been unlucky.

I married my husband on 17 March 1927. I was 21 and my husband was 29. There was somebody who arranged things for us, and my husband came to my grandparents' house to take a look at me. Within 20 days we got married, so I had no idea what sort of man he was. I hadn't even seen his face properly. My Grandad just kept on saying:

'He's a good man! He's a good man! You should marry him! You should marry him!'

I said, 'All right,' and that's how it was decided. In those days, if you started to hum and ha, your parents would scold you and call you selfish.

The wedding ceremony was in the evening. I was wearing a white bridal *kimono* and a floss silk veil. My Granny told me:

'You're leaving this house for good now. Once you take off the floss silk veil at the house where you're going as a bride, that will become the place for you to die.'

She also said: 'You can't come and live at this house any more. A woman mustn't come and go as she pleases. Wherever she is, a woman must put up with things. However unhappy you might be, you mustn't grumble. Wherever she is, a woman's life is full of tears.'

As she said this, my Granny was crying herself. Since they were the words of my Granny, who'd brought me up, I just kept saying 'Yes' as I listened to her.

I thought to myself that, whatever happened, I would have to put up with it. I remember how sad I felt, wearing my bridal clothes, as I listened to my Granny. My parents, and my brothers and sisters, were all in Hawaii. I was so upset at having to get married, after my hopes of going to Hawaii had been dashed, that it almost broke my heart. Nowadays, even if they're married, girls can run away or whatever, if they're unhappy. In the old days, it was hammered into our heads what a wife should be like, and that's what we believed when we got married.

Eijirō was a gentle person. He was a steady type and people liked him. After he was killed by the atom bomb, people often used to joke with me, saying:

'Your "Ee" [abbreviation of Eijirō] was an "ee" [meaning "good"] man. I bet you can't forget him!'

On the farm, we had 3 *tan* [about ³/₄ acre] of dry land and 1 *tan* 5 *se* [about ³/₈ acre] of paddy fields. Since it was mainly dry farming, we were always busy. Together with my husband, I threw myself into the work. This is a *mouli*-growing district. In winter we grew a lot of *mouli* for pickling, and in summer we grew a lot of burdock. People used to say that Kami Nukui *mouli* was fine-grained and tasty, and that our burdock was so white and tender that it wasn't a bit stringy.

My husband used to load the vegetables on to a boat and take them to the fruit and vegetable market in Ōtemachi. As for me, I'd be washing the *mouli* and burdock until late into the night. I'd get up at 1 o'clock in the morning, pack up two meals for my husband and see him off. He'd eat breakfast when he got to the market. Then he'd load up the boat with nightsoil and in the afternoon, when the wind from the south sprung up, he'd come back. He'd eat the dinner I'd packed up for him on the boat.

In those days, you could build a good house for as little as ¥1000. The profit on vegetables wasn't all that great, but it was hard cash all the same, so we all jumped on the bandwagon.

We raised a lot of silkworms too. That was hard work! Silkworms are all mouth, so there were nights when I wouldn't get a wink of sleep, looking after them. In spring, I could often raise them pretty well, but in summer, because it was hot, I often failed. In the rainy season, if I fed them wet mulberry leaves, they'd get *umiko* disease and wouldn't spin any cocoons. Or they'd get *atamasuki* disease; in that case, they'd only spin tiny cocoons, which you couldn't sell.

If even one of them became *umiko*, it would soon spread to the others. That was why it was hard work looking after them. From silkworms too we could get hard cash, so that was another bandwagon that we all jumped on. Even so, I never spent a penny on myself. Another problem was that if I spent all my time on the silkworms, I couldn't get on with the weeding, and then the fields would end up choked with weeds.

With Seiji (the eldest son) strapped on my back, I was the one who looked after the silkworms. I had to, because my husband was away during the day, collecting nightsoil. It was hard doing the work with a baby on your back. But if I put him down and left him, he'd cry. Taking advantage of the dark room, I'd have a good cry as I fed the silkworms their mulberry leaves, with Seiji on my back. Time and again, I felt that I'd like to go back to my grandparents.

Our food was really poor. It was rice mixed with barley. Sometimes my husband came back on the boat with some fish that he'd bought. They'd be salted mackerel or sardines. We ate a lot of vegetables. We grew millet and ate it as dumplings. Thinking to myself that things would be easier when the kids grew up, I'd work on.

My husband's fateful words

When they dropped the atom bomb, our eldest boy, Seiji, was in the second year at the Railway College in Mihara. He must have been 15. Our second boy was called Teruo. He's the one I'm living with now. He was 7 at the time. Like I said before, our third boy, Hideaki, was 2. What with a baby at my breast and two growing lads, it was really hard.

My husband often used to take the horse and cart and go to Hiroshima to collect nightsoil. He'd say:

'I often go to Hiroshima. There's no knowing when I might be killed in an air raid . . .'

He said the same thing on the morning of the 6th. I told him: 'Don't tempt fate! It upsets me. Why are you always saying that sort of thing?'

He said: 'What I mean is, you never know when I might be caught by an air raid. So don't be surprised if I'm killed.'

I said: 'With three children, what would happen to us all without you? It upsets me. Surely you don't have to say that sort of thing as you're setting off in the morning . . .?'

He said: 'Today's the 6th. I might come back after loading up the timber from the houses that we were dismantling up till yesterday. Or I might go with the others to see a film. In that case, I'll be late . . . You could get Kumi (a daughter of one of the neighbours and a member of the Volunteer Corps) to bring my lunch box . . .'

It was about 2 o'clock in the morning when my husband, Kenzō Tochimura and the others set off with the ox-cart. Each time he'd come back after dismantling houses, he'd brought some timber with him, and we'd used it for building a hut, and as firewood for heating the bath. Mr Tochimura had a big, strong ox and that was why they'd decided to take the ox-cart. But oxen don't like the hot sun, so they had to set off early in the morning, in order to get back while it was still cool.

Mr Tochimura loaded up the timber at Nakajima and then came back early, before the atom bomb was dropped. My husband stayed behind and carried on with the work of dismantling buildings. When he got back, Mr Tochimura said to me:

'I told them I was sorry that after they'd set off so early in the morning, they still had to stay on and work late . . .'

On the morning of the 6th, I was feeding the baby and clearing up. Teruo had a boil and I was thinking of taking him to Imai Clinic in Midorii. Just then, there was a blinding flash, followed almost immediately by a big BANG. I thought it was strange and wondered if there was a firework display somewhere. But following the flash, it was as though a black curtain had been hung over my eyes and several times I waved my hand, trying to brush it aside. I couldn't even see my children, so for a moment I panicked. Sliding doors tumbled down and the *shōji* screens were smashed. It was made worse because the doors were all shut. The ceiling was pushed up as well.

When I went outside to take a look, there were flames and smoke billowing up into the sky over Hiroshima. I became uneasy, thinking to myself: 'What's happened? Has something happened to Hiroshima?'

It was just gone noon when a neighbour, who worked at Yoshijima Prison, told me: 'The Kawauchi Volunteer Corps has been wiped out.'

After a while, somebody else said: 'The survivors are going to be brought back by lorry.'

Hearing that, I ran to the Hironaka shop nearby. They were calling out names, but mine wasn't called. Then somebody said that we should go to Yutani. With Hideaki on my back, I pulled the cart there, but there was no sign of my husband. Next I went to the river embankment, because people said a boat was due to bring back survivors there. Pulling the cart behind me, I tried one place after another. Hideaki stayed quietly on my back the whole time.

I expected my husband to get back safely, but he didn't come. It didn't seem likely that he'd even eaten the lunch which Kumi had taken for him, because she didn't come back either.

That night was so sad and lonely. I can't put it into words. Thinking to myself that he might get back at any time, I didn't sleep, but just kept on peering out into the yard. I was still believing he would come back. I longed for him to come back. It's just not possible to tell you how I felt that night.

'Daddy! Over there! Bang!'

On the morning of the 7th, I didn't feel like doing anything. I just went out to the embankment round the back of the house to take a look. I was thinking to myself that perhaps he'd come limping home, on burnt legs, or something like that . . .

I was like a cat on hot bricks. I couldn't bear just doing nothing, so after putting an air-raid hood on Hideaki, I strapped him on my back and set off to look for my husband in Hiroshima. I was wearing a pair of straw sandals that my husband had made. Passing through Ōshiba, I hurried on to Aioi Bridge. I walked along the riverbank, stopping to look closely at each dead body. I was thinking to myself that maybe he'd died at the riverside with his head slumped into the water, or that his body might be floating in the water and trapped against the bank.

The sun came up and made it hot. On top of that, the bombed ruins of the town were still smouldering and that added to the heat. Hiroshima was like a flaming hell. The factories and the roads were still on fire. My straw sandals were worn out on the way there. Hideaki was saying: 'Hot! . . . hot!' and it really must have been hot for him, strapped on my back. Another thing he'd say was: 'Milk! . . . milk!' All I could think about was finding my husband, so even though he asked for milk again and again, I pretended not to hear. Shifting his position on my back, I'd walk on.

When I got to Aioi Bridge, a policeman asked me: 'What have you come for?'

I said: 'My husband went off with the Volunteer Corps and hasn't come back. I've come to look for him because I thought his body might be in the river, trapped against the bank or something like that.'

He stopped me from going on, saying: 'From here on it gets dangerous, so you mustn't go. Especially with a baby on your back, you can't go on. You must turn back.'

There was nothing I could do, so I walked back towards Sōtoku Middle School and Ōshiba to see if my husband was round there. Around Chōjūen, a lot of soldiers from the Engineering Corps had died. They'd tumbled down the riverbank . . . They were covered in burns, with bulging eyeballs, and their bodies were swollen and had turned a purple colour. The skin on their hands was in tatters and hung down from their fingertips. They were all youngsters, about 20 years old. Their uniforms had been burnt off their backs, so that only their fronts were clothed. It was heartbreaking to see them. In the river too, there were a lot of dead soldiers whose bodies had been brought up on the high tide.

On the river embankment, there were people who were still alive. Some of them were stretching out hands that were all peeled, with the skin hanging off in tatters. They were saying:

'Give me some water, Mum! Help me, Mum! Water!'

There were hundreds of dead bodies in the bamboo wood at Ōshiba. Some were lying face up, others face down. It was terrible to see so many dead youngsters. I'll never forget the sight of those poor people. It was the horrible war which had done it. It was so sad. Tears were streaming down my face and I couldn't stop them.

I searched all over, but my husband wasn't anywhere. At the edge of the bamboo wood at Ōshiba, I took the baby off my back and gave him my breast. The sun had already gone down. In that bamboo wood, there were a lot of people, some already dead, others injured. The air was full of groaning voices. My straw sandals had fallen to pieces. Dragging my feet, I went back home, where my second boy had grown tired of waiting for me. I was worn out . . .

On the morning of the 8th, I made some rice balls. Teruo was in the second year of elementary school and I said to him:

'I'm going to look for Dad, so you be a good boy while I'm away.'

Taking a spare pair of *ashinaka* straw sandals with me, I set off about 6 o'clock. I left Teruo all on his own and he did well, keeping an eye on the house for me. Like everybody else, he had to put up with a lot at that time.

It was a long way to Hiroshima. Nowadays, there's nobody walks that far. But in those days, I went all the way there to search for my husband, without even thinking about how far it was or how hot it was. And I had a baby on my back . . . I'd pat Hideaki every time he said 'Hot, hot!' or 'Milk, milk!' I walked all the way along the riverbank, searching for my husband the whole time. I was wondering whether his body might be trapped against the riverbank somewhere, or whether it could have been brought up on the high tide that far. I've never seen so many dead bodies! Flies had settled everywhere. It was heartbreaking to see dead bodies in that state. Thinking to myself that my husband might be among them, I checked any number of those dead bodies as I walked along.

On my back, Hideaki kept saying 'Hot!' and 'Milk!' Later he started raising his arms and saying:
'Daddy! Over there! Bang!'
I'd been trying to comfort him, by telling him:
'That bang's made Daddy go away. Let's look for him. So you put up with this heat, eh?'
That was why he started saying: 'Daddy! Over there! Bang!'
Whenever he said 'Bang!', he'd kick out his legs and raise his arms up. On the morning of the 9th too, I set off early to search for my husband. On my back, I took with me 'Daddy! Over there! Bang!' . . .
Perhaps I was the only one at that time who took a baby with her to search for her husband. A lot of women were widowed and left with children, but they had old people, or at least somebody at home to look after the children. I didn't have anybody like that, so all I could do was leave 7-year-old Teruo to look after the house and strap the baby on my back when I went off searching. For some time afterwards, the neighbours used to say to me:
'How did you manage, with a baby on your back?'
When at last I'd get back home after the sun had gone down, I'd be dog tired. I'd hug Teruo, who'd been looking after the house for me and, without thinking, I'd grumble, 'Hasn't Dad come back yet . . .?' and start to cry. For three days I walked all over, searching for my husband, but there wasn't a sign of him anywhere. There was nothing I could do.

I didn't know where to begin the farming

I couldn't find my husband even after three days of searching for him and he didn't come back either. He didn't come back then, so he won't ever come back now. I thought that if I could set eyes even on his dead body, I'd get some peace of mind. But no trace of him was ever found. For three days I searched in vain. Dead or alive, I never found him. That will weigh on my mind for ever.
People say that there's no point in talking to the dead, but I don't think so. He never came back, but that still doesn't stop me from talking to Dad. I talk to his photograph. I say:
'I went again and again to look for you. I'm sorry, but I couldn't find you.'
That's what I say, but of course he can't answer me. Other times, I say: 'Where are you, dear? You went through hell, dear. It must have been terrible.'

When I kneel in front of the household altar to the Buddha and look at his photograph, I find myself saying:
'You might feel that nobody cares for you, dear. But I'll look after you . . .'
That's what I say when I look at his photograph. Even now, I still keep on talking to him, as though we were together only yesterday.

If I go on and on, talking about my husband, you might think that it's a man I need, but if I hadn't talked so much to my dead husband, I couldn't have put up with things like I have all these years. My husband left home for the last time on the morning of the 6th and he never came back. He was the person that I relied on, and he suddenly disappeared. I think I've done well to get through all these years since then. It's talking to my dead husband's photograph that's helped me to pull through.

For a while, I didn't feel like working. Before I knew it, the fields were full of weeds. The cucumbers had shrivelled up. I was on edge, because I didn't know what to do. All I could think about was that I had to bring up my children and not let them fall into bad ways. I wanted to bring them up so that people would never say: 'Their mother's a widow and that's why they're wild kids.'

I used to say to the boys:
'Even though your Dad's not here, he can see what you're doing. Be good lads and don't get into trouble . . .'

After several days had passed, Seiji, who was in the Railway College at Mihara, came back home without warning. He told me:
'Dad's dead and I'm the eldest son, so I've got to look after everything from now on. I've decided to leave school and come home.'

It was so sudden, I was shocked. I said to him:
'It would be better to carry on and finish your schooling . . .'

I really thought it would be better for him to finish his studies. Of course, I was pleased that he'd come back home and for his saying that he'd take over from Dad, but even though he talked about going to collect nightsoil, he was still young and not fully grown. It was too much for him. All the same, I was grateful for his saying: 'I'll take over from Dad . . .'

Night and day, all I could think about was how I could feed my three boys and bring them up to be fully grown men. I did everything I could to make sure that they kept to the straight and narrow, and that they didn't get into trouble.

The farmwork was a real strain. When my husband was alive, I'd

just done as he said, so when I found myself on my own, I didn't
know where to begin. My husband had often used an ox, but I didn't
know how to handle one, so there was nothing else for it but to hoe
the soil by hand.

On the other side of the River Ōta we had 1 *tan* 5 *se* [about ³/₈
acre] of paddy fields in what is now Kōyō Town. My husband and I
used to go there to grow rice. Since there was no bridge, my husband
used to take us across by boat. But after he died, there was no one
who could handle the boat, so I had to go across on the ferry to get
to our land.

Working hard like that, I grew what I thought was enough rice to
feed us, but then we had to hand it all over to the authorities. That
really got me down. I thought to myself that if that was the way
things were, it would be better to be dead like Dad. It was so
frustrating. I just couldn't hold back the tears.

Because the boys were small, I couldn't go to collect nightsoil
either. Without fertiliser, we ended up not being able to grow even
enough to feed ourselves. Again and again, we had to deliver what
we grew to the authorities, so we were left with hardly anything to
eat in the house. It was so frustrating and miserable that I lost count
of the number of times I shed tears.

Even the weeds treated me badly

We had to hand over to the authorities nearly all the good crops, so
all that remained for us were the leftovers. With growing lads on my
hands, there was nothing so painful as not having enough to eat.

Instead of proper rice and barley, we were given a ration of reject
potatoes and foreign rice. And I remember that once we got some
mouldy dried noodles. If we had thrown them away because they
were mouldy, we wouldn't have had anything to eat. So we boiled
them up and tried to eat them, but they were so mouldy that we just
couldn't stomach them.

Another time we got a ration of salted mackerel. Thinking to
myself that this time they'd given us something decent, I opened
them up and to my horror found they were full of maggots. I'd been
thinking how happy the boys would be to sit down to eat them . . .
However short of food we were, we couldn't eat maggot-ridden
mackerel!

The boys had good appetites, but food was always short and after
every meal they were still hungry. I'd get some little potatoes, boil

them up, and the boys would eat them with salt. When we had a lot of pumpkins, I'd cut them up, boil them, wrap them in dough, and roast them on the fire. Or I'd mash the pumpkins and use them as filling for steamed dumplings. We used to eat them day after day. At one stage, both the boys and I were undernourished and got really thin. After the atom bomb was dropped, for the best part of ten years we somehow kept ourselves alive by eating all sorts.

Until the youngest boy, Hideaki, got to be about 10, life was really hard. It was a big job just turning whatever odds and ends of food I could lay my hands on into proper meals. As I scraped together their meals, it was always on my mind that I mustn't let them start stealing from other people because they were hungry.

In ragged clothes, I put all my effort into bringing up the boys and doing the farmwork. I never went out anywhere. Even when the others asked me to go with them, I couldn't manage to. I never had any new clothes made either. Anyway, if you're wearing good clothes, you can't work on a farm. Because of the war, I had a really miserable time. Yes, I had a really hard time.

Even when we grew vegetables, they weren't good enough for selling. Even when we grew burdock, the roots were no thicker than chopsticks. We didn't have any nightsoil or compost to spread on the soil, so you couldn't expect anything better.

One of the neighbours was at Saijō Agricultural College (Saijō Prefectural Agricultural High School in East Hiroshima) and once I asked him what was the best way to grow good crops. I told him: 'Our burdock doesn't grow well.'

And he said: 'Your soil's grown poor. All the life has gone out of it.'

We hadn't been putting nightsoil back into the ground and we couldn't afford to buy any either. Since the atom bomb was dropped, we hadn't put any sort of fertiliser into the ground. So I could accept what he said, that our soil hadn't got any life in it. Yet although vegetables wouldn't grow, weeds seemed to thrive. Being a farming widow, even the weeds treated me badly!

Nowadays, my daughter-in-law and me farm 1 *tan* 5 *se* [³/₈ acre] of dry land. I don't work as hard as I used to in the old days, but when I'm indoors I start worrying about the crops. Even on rainy days, if I stay indoors, I get uneasy. Going out into the fields has become part of me, so even on rainy days I don't stay at home.

My children try to stop me. They say:

'Don't go out in the fields. Take it easy!'

But I'm not the type to take it easy. As long as I live, I'll work on the farm. Work is my lifeblood now. Work is part of my flesh and bones. People tell me not to work, but if I did what they said, I wouldn't last more than a day or two. As long as I can keep on working, I will.

I tell my grandchildren about their Grandad who was killed by the atom bomb. When I give them some pocket money, I say to them:

'This money is from your Grandad. It's not from me. Go over to where Grandad is (the Buddhist household altar) and say a prayer.'

My grandchildren listen carefully to what I tell them, and I hear them saying:

'It's because of Grandad's suffering that I'm getting this money. Thank you, Grandad!'

There's nothing in his grave. We couldn't find any trace of him. He didn't come back then, so he'll never come back now. I'm resigned to it.

But all the same, hasn't my husband come back here (the family grave)? After all, there's nowhere else for him to go, is there? Really, it was a terrible war!

Even now, I pray at his grave, believing he's here. Just this morning, I put some rape blossoms on his grave.

15　Haru Takasaki

15 We've Lived This Long by Encouraging One Another
Haru Takasaki

I was called a traitor

The place where I was born was Tsubuse, in Minuchi Village, in Saeki District. Nowadays, as you know, it's called Yuki. We didn't have that much land, but we were landlords, on top of which we farmed about 5 *tan* [1¼ acres] ourselves. My mother had trouble with her legs, so her parents adopted a son-in-law (my father) from Kuchi Village, in Asa District, to do the farming. In our house we had four or five employees – farmhands, farmlads and maids. They did all the farming and housework, so I don't ever remember doing any farmwork when I was a child.

For the maids, we bought rice-planting clothes in May, a summer *kimono* and *obi* [sash] at the *Bon* Festival, and a pretty *kimono* at New Year. We didn't pay them a penny in wages, but in that way they prepared themselves for marriage. In those days, there were lots of village girls who went into domestic service. The men got their food and were given some rice too.

I was born on 17 February 1902. I had one older brother. After he'd finished Teachers' Training College in Hiroshima, he became a teacher at Miyauchi Elementary School (in Saeki District). But he died from influenza when he was only 28. As for me, I kept good health. After attending the Branch School of Minuchi Elementary School up to the third year, I moved to Minuchi Shimo Elementary School, which was about 1 *ri* [about 4 kilometres] from home. After three years there, I entered Minuchi Higher Elementary School. In those days, going to higher elementary school was like going to university now, so only about three girls from my elementary school carried on to higher elementary school. All the others went into domestic service. After leaving higher elementary school, I went to a place in Teramachi, in Hiroshima, where they taught *kimono*-making.

In those days, there were lots of boats going up and down the River Ōta. In the spring of my sixteenth year, I went to Hiroshima on a boat which was loaded up with firewood and charcoal. My parents had rented an upstairs room near to Teramachi for me and I learnt *kimono*-making for two years. When I went home, I used to take the light railway as far as Kabe and get off at Furuichibashi. From there, I'd sometimes get on a rickshaw pulled by dogs, but since I didn't have money to throw around, I'd often walk. I'd go from Furuichibashi to Kuchi Village, and then go over the Hagiwara Pass. . . I'd go up and down the mountain paths for a good 5 *ri* [about 20 kilometres] and eventually arrive home. And that was wearing a *kimono* and *geta* clogs! . . . When there was snow on the ground, the bottom of my *kimono* would be frozen stiff. In those days, if you said you were studying *kimono*-making in Hiroshima, people thought you were a lucky girl.

In 1923, I came here to get married. My husband's family were landlords too. On the dry land, we grew a lot of millet; and we grew quite a lot of vegetables, like *mouli* and carrots, for selling, so we were kept pretty busy.

My husband was called Masaru. He was a gentle soul, an honest type, of few words. He was nine years older than me. He must have been born in 1893. We brought up three children. Our son was called Yutaka. When he was in the third year of Saijō Agricultural College, he came back one day and told me:

'Mum, the college wants me to go on the preparatory course for the Fleet Air Arm.'

I thought that he ought to finish college first, so straightaway I went to the college and said:

'Please don't put ideas into my boy's head like soon applying for a studentship for the Fleet Air Arm. Please let him finish his studies at college.'

Later I heard from Yutaka that the teachers at the college said to him: 'Your mother is a traitor!' I think it's a good thing that I was a traitor! If I'd let Yutaka join the Fleet Air Arm, he wouldn't be alive today.

Our elder daughter, Miyoko, finished school and at the time when they dropped the atom bomb, she was doing clerical work for the Akatsuki Corps and had been assigned to Kawauchi Elementary School. When the pupils were mobilised, our younger daughter, Fumie, was sent to the Hiroshima Savings Office. That's where she was when they dropped the atom bomb nearby.

My husband was chairman of the neighbourhood association, so on the morning of the 6th, he assembled everybody and set off on foot with a fireman's axe over his shoulder. They all went off hale and hearty, with my husband saying:

'Today's the last day of dismantling buildings, so we're planning to finish by mid-day. I'll be back early . . .'

The village girls went off in good spirits too, saying:

'Today's the last day. When we finish, we'll go and see a film.'

Nobody imagined that morning that a terrible fate awaited them in the form of the atom bomb. Even now I can hear their voices as they went off, saying:

'Bye-bye. See you later!'

My daughter came back covered in blood

After seeing off my husband, I cleared up in the kitchen and then went out into the field at the front of the house. We were growing a lot of millet, so with my hoe I was banking up earth around the roots. First there was a blinding flash; and then, after what seemed like ten minutes, there was a big BANG. A lot of oil drums had been brought to the Hachiman Shrine nearby and left there. I thought it was them that had exploded.

When I went into the house to take a look, everything had tumbled down. Doors and *shōji* screens had been sent flying and the ceiling had been pushed up. I'd set out a meal for Yutaka on the household altar, as a prayer for his safe return, but soot had fallen from the straw-thatched roof and the food was black as coal. About 10 o'clock, the loudspeaker announced:

'The Volunteer Corps from Kawauchi is reported to have been wiped out.'

I talked about the announcement with our neighbours, and we told each other:

'They can't be wiped out . . .'

We all thought it couldn't be anything more than incendiary bombs that had been dropped.

Fumie came back about 11 o'clock, covered in blood. She was in the fourth year at the Girls' Higher School and after the pupils had been mobilised, she'd been working at the Savings Office. Her workplace was on the fourth floor of the annexe of the former Fukuya Department Store and she felt the direct effects of the atom bomb there. They were all badly injured. I heard that she first went to

Hiroshima Station, with her friend from Hesaka, and that from there they fled eastwards. If at that time they'd fled to the west (in the direction of the epicentre of the atom bomb), they'd almost certainly have died in the fires.

Splinters of broken glass were stuck, like prickles in a hedgehog, all over her head and shoulders. She and her friend had helped each other to get back, and she said that blood from her friend had got on to her too. She looked terrible. I said:

'You did well to get back.'

And she said:

'It's terrible in Hiroshima.'

While I was looking after Fumie, a stream of burnt people, who were fleeing from Hiroshima, started to come by. With their skin hanging off them, they all looked like ghosts . . .

Even when it grew dark, my husband didn't come back. I thought to myself:

'Since he hasn't come back, he must be looking after the injured or helping the refugees. That's why he hasn't got back . . .'

Thinking along those lines, I waited. A rescue party from Nakachōshi set off by boat to pick up those who were still alive who had managed to get back as far as Misasa Embankment. Somebody said that my husband might come back on that boat, so I put a change of clothes and some bandages into the cart, and I was just thinking about setting off when the air-raid warning sounded. Whenever the all-clear sounded and I'd think once more about setting off, the air-raid warning would sound again . . . I can't tell you what that night was like. Two or three people who were still alive, and about ten dead bodies, were brought back on the boat, but my husband wasn't among them. The Nakachōshi people told us:

'We don't know where the others are, or what has happened to them.'

That night I nursed Fumie, having dimmed the light because I was scared by the air-raid warnings.

The next day, I started to search for my husband. On the road, people were walking along like ghosts and there were burnt and charred bodies lying about on the verges. The dead bodies were all swollen up like the Deva Kings. When I peered into the air-raid shelters, there were lots of dead bodies piled up, one on top of the other. Among them were some people who were still alive. 'Give me some water; water . . .' they were saying. In the river, there were many bloated dead bodies too. Lots of them were little more than middle-school children . . . Bodies were piled up on the steps leading down to the river. I suppose they'd gone down the steps to take a drink of water and died there. The sight of those dead bodies was enough to break your heart.

My husband's Volunteer Corps had left their lunch boxes at the Seigan Temple in Nakajima Shinmachi. Then they'd got on with the work of dismantling houses so as to make fire-breaks. I thought to myself that I must somehow or other get to the place where my husband and his friends had been working. I pressed on into the city centre, but it had been placed under martial law. They stopped me and I was told:

'You can't go any further!'

But when I explained the reason, they let me go on. Near to the Seigan Temple, Tatsujirō Fujioka (Kiyono Fujioka's husband) was lying dead. With a charred stick, I wrote 'Tatsujirō Fujioka' on a stone at the side of him. Nearby there was a man who was still alive. I said to him:

'Tell me your name. I'll write your name down, so tell me what it is.'

Again and again I asked him, but he didn't utter a word. In the end, I couldn't find any trace of my husband on that day. It grew dark and when I turned back home, the rice warehouse in Misasa was on fire, with flames being thrown up into the sky.

The next day too, I set off early, determined to find my husband. All the dead bodies were burnt black and looked the same. It occurred to me that however many bodies I looked at as I walked along, I wouldn't be able to recognise my husband. Then I remembered a peculiar thing about my husband's finger. His fingernail had broken and there was a crack in it. So I decided to look out for that as I searched. But even though I searched all morning, I didn't find him. There were thousands, and even tens of thousands, of bodies. It was hot and I sank down weakly at the roadside. I felt so helpless. Even if I'd wanted to cry, the tears wouldn't have come. I was beyond tears. All I wanted to do was to cry out at the top of my voice: 'Dad!'

Working for the Atom Bomb Widows' Association

Even though I searched for three or four days, I couldn't find my husband. Hiroshima was like a living hell and I started to think that he couldn't still be alive there. I thought he might have fled to the river and died there. Perhaps he had disappeared without trace because his body had been swept away by the current. Thinking like that, I'd tell myself that I had to come to terms with his death, but of course I couldn't come to terms with it.

Since he didn't come back, we couldn't have a funeral. Returning to the village after searching in vain, I'd see lots of bodies being cremated by the riverside, with the flames lighting up the night sky. But I didn't have a single thing of his to burn.

At the beginning of September, Yutaka was discharged from the Marine Corps on Shōdo Island (in Kagawa Prefecture). He came back without knowing that his father was missing. He was 19 at the time. After Yutaka came back, I started to feel like working again.

In those days, nightsoil was the only fertiliser we had. If you didn't go to collect nightsoil, you couldn't grow any crops. Yutaka would get up at 1 or 2 o'clock in the morning and go to collect nightsoil. We got in touch with various relatives in Ujina and made arrangements to collect their nightsoil. Yutaka would bring back three tubfuls on the cart. I'd estimate when Yutaka would reach Furuichibashi and I'd go to meet him there and help him to push the cart. Yutaka would be pulling the cart that was loaded with nightsoil and I never heard a single grumble from him. He worked really hard at collecting nightsoil and I felt grateful to him as I helped push the cart. Washing out the nightsoil tub was my job. I'd wash it clean and get things ready for Yutaka to go off the next morning. We went halves with Mr Nishimoto next door and bought a horse. After we started using a horse and cart, things got much easier. Then in 1952 we bought a three-wheeled truck. From then on, we didn't have to get up in the middle of the night any more and I could retire as a cart-pusher! After the atom bomb was dropped, for about three years we couldn't grow very good crops. For about ten years, we had a really hard time.

In 1949 we found a husband for Miyoko and in 1950 Yutaka took a wife. Soon after that, we found a husband for Fumie too, so although times were hard, I managed to get both my daughters married. I couldn't lay on splendid weddings, because in those days alcohol and clothes were rationed and in short supply. But, being a widow, I made a big effort and did all the things that parents should do for their children.

Yutaka thought that there was nobody except him to get on with the farming, so he really worked hard for us all. In 1950 he became chairman of the Young Farmers' League and, although he was still young, he became a member of the Town Assembly. As for me, I've been working for the Widows' Association, which was formed on 4

February 1949. We gave it the name 'Shiraumekai' (White Plum Blossom Association). The chairwoman was Chiyono Nishimura (now 85 years old) and I became the deputy-chairwoman. Later I was made chairwoman.

In order to get a cash income for our members, we made arrangements for widows to do work in their homes for various companies. We also collected money and from our funds made loans to those in need, with the officials of the Widows' Association acting as the guarantors. We thought that everybody needed to get away and let off steam once in a while, so we arranged various outings, such as gathering shellfish on the beach at low tide and a trip to the hot springs at Beppu. We tried to provide both material and moral support for the widows. For those who'd lost their husbands when the atom bomb was dropped, taking part in the meetings of the Widows' Association was the one chance they had to relax.

I also work for the Women's Buddhist Association at Jyōgyō Temple. Our husbands died on 6 August, so on the 6th of every month we all gather at the temple and get the priest to chant a sutra. Even listening to a sutra can't take away the sadness we feel over the death of our husbands, but going to the temple, seeing the faces of other widows like ourselves, and chatting with them, is the best medicine there is. When you go there and see that somebody is doing well, you think to yourself that you've got to pull yourself together too for your children's sake. Or if you hear somebody talking about getting a husband for her daughter, you think that you mustn't let her do better than you. So we look upon our gatherings on the 6th as occasions for bolstering up our spirits.

We were all sisters whose lives were suddenly turned upside down by the atom bomb, so we lived on by encouraging one another. We were all working on the land and, somehow, we all managed to survive. Nowadays, we're all happy. As for myself, I do the farmwork with my daughter-in-law and I feel grateful to be spending my last days in happiness. For us old folks, the nicest thing is to be doing what we like best – working on the land.

16   Midori Matsumoto

16 Even Now There Are Nights When I Can't Sleep

Midori Matsumoto

He took some cooked beans with him

Today I'm seeing to the spinach. I was born on 8 April 1898. I'll be 83 this year, but I still work hard on the farm. I can't get rid of the habit of working. My daughter-in-law tells me to take it easy, but as long as I can manage to, I'll keep on working. Once a month, when I feel like it, I go to Sōgo (a department store in Hiroshima). I like department stores. 'I'll take care,' I tell my family, and off I go.

'Midori', my name, is officially written in old-fashioned letters. Wherever I go, people find it difficult to read. For everyday use I write it in modern letters. Anyway, my parents' house was in Kogomori, in Fuchū, in Aki District. My father was employed at the Central Post Office in Hiroshima. I was the eldest child and I had two younger brothers. I had never done any farmwork.

I got married in the autumn of 1916, when I was 18. A relative of ours in Midorii said to me:

'Life will be easy there, so marry their son.'

When I got married, I was surprised to find that they grew a lot of Kyō greens. Not only that, but they grew a lot of grain. They had 2 *tan* [about ¹/₂ acre] of paddy fields and 5 *tan* [about 1¹/₄ acres] of dry land. They grew barley, millet and some crops that I'd never seen before. When I tried sowing seeds, I found that I couldn't sow them in the proper way, using the palm of my hand, and sometimes I was near to tears. We used to grow indigo plants on 2 *tan* of dry land alongside the embankment. We grew hemp as well. In summer the hemp grew so thick that it was almost like being in the dark when you walked between the rows. They used to grow a lot of hemp on all the farms, and a lot of barley too.

Anyhow, never having done it before, the farmwork really gave me a lot of trouble. To start with, I didn't even know the names of the crops that I was looking after. I'd get up while it was still dark, so that I hardly knew whether I was asleep or awake. We were always busy, but so was everybody else, and if you didn't work, people would just laugh at you. Until I got used to it, there were times when I was in a daze, and my husband often used to get angry with me. But you're bound to be in a daze sometimes when you don't know what's going on!

We used to eat rice mixed with barley. We were a small household. There was my husband's grandfather, Heisuke; my husband's father, Seiichi; and my husband. With me, that made four. So our food was better than average. There was no time to rest, even after eating. From morning till night, I was forever weeding. My husband was called Shigeo and he was five years older than me. He was 53 when the atom bomb was dropped. He was highly regarded and a member of the Village Assembly. He was always ready to listen to people and everyone in the village trusted him.

On the morning of the 6th, he said to me:

'Everybody's worked well. Can you cook a lot of mottled kidney beans, so that I can take plenty along for everyone?'

I cooked a lot, seasoned with salt.

He was one of the Volunteer Corps' officials, so he was very busy with jobs like checking the numbers and keeping in touch with the office. He couldn't spare much time for the farmwork, so I had to work very hard. My husband was the type who looked after other people and he must have been pleased with everyone's cooperation. That's why he set off early, taking the cooked beans with him.

Since my husband set off early that day, I started weeding the paddy field early as well. The rice plants were growing nicely. While I was weeding the paddy field, I raised my head and saw a B29 passing over. I felt uneasy, thinking that it might drop some bombs. As soon as I felt the blinding flash, there was an enormous BANG. I threw myself face down in the paddy field, wondering what on earth had happened. While I was staring blankly, Kiyono Fujioka from next door called out:

'You should see your house! It's fallen to bits!'

I hurried home to see what the matter was. The doors and everything had crashed down. The windows were broken and glass was scattered everywhere. And the ceiling had been pushed up. It was a right old mess. I thought to myself that my husband would fix things when he got back. But when I went into the yard to take a look, everything was black over towards Hiroshima. From the direction of Hiroshima, a sort of white bag (the parachute used to drop the atom bomb) came floating over. The neighbours were running here and there, asking each other what had happened. I didn't feel like doing any more work, but I didn't feel like going into the house either.

Our elder boy, Shigeyuki, had gone off to the war and we'd got word that he was somewhere in the Philippines. Our younger boy, Toshio, had been called up into the Hiroshima Division, but because he was ill, he'd been evacuated to a hospital in Ōda, in Shimane Prefecture. That's why, as it turned out, he wasn't in Hiroshima when the atom bomb was dropped. There were just the two of us, my husband and me, left at home. When it happened, I was on my own, so although the whole house was upside down, there was nothing I could do.

My husband and my elder son come back in my dreams

About mid-day, the injured started to come back. As evening came on, it was reported:

'The Volunteer Corps has been wiped out.'

I felt really helpless. That night my husband didn't come back.

From the 7th, for about a week, I went out searching for my husband. Together with other women whose husbands hadn't come back, I walked all over. On the 7th, flames were still rising from over towards the Western Drill Ground. I'd got no idea where he could be. A lot of people had died, still clinging to the railings of Misasa Bridge. They were burnt black and their skin had peeled and was hanging off them . . . Many dead bodies were floating underneath the bridge too. As I passed by, injured people would beg me:

'Give me some water! Give me some water!'

I went every day to Aioi Bridge and walked around, carefully checking the corpses. There weren't any corpses floating in the water there. I suppose the current had carried them off.

It must have been about the 10th that someone came to see me from the village office. They said:

'A dead body has been found near by Yoshijima Prison. Although it's infested with maggots, it looks like your husband. Please go and see.'

I thought my husband had been found, so I flew over there to see, but it was somebody different. Maggots were spilling out of the body. It was really scary.

Even though I searched for a whole week, there was no sign of my husband. I'd get back home, tired out with walking, but with nothing to show for it. Meanwhile, the people who'd come back covered with burns died one after another.

The house was upside down, my husband hadn't come back and I couldn't sleep much. The Fujiokas next door were relatives of ours and when they asked me to stay with them, I took advantage of their offer. I stayed with the Fujiokas for about ten days, but I couldn't stay there for ever. Somehow I cleared up the mess in the house and moved back in. Being a woman on my own, I'd get scared going out round the back of the house when night came on. But even so, there'd be nights when I'd feel that my husband had come back unexpectedly, and I'd go out and walk round the house.

On hot summer nights, my husband would appear in my dreams, wearing his *hanten* jacket. Silently, he'd look at me. Time and again, I'd jump up, thinking he'd come back. But however long I waited, he didn't come back. Even now there are days when I'm on edge, thinking he's alive somewhere.

All on my own, one lonely day followed another. It was so miserable, with the house still unrepaired. But do you know, in those days there weren't any bad people to frighten you.

Some of our relatives came to stay, for one reason or another, like having been burnt out. My younger boy was demobbed too, so there were more of us in the house. We kept ourselves alive, living on whatever food there was.

Since the war was over, I was thinking to myself that my elder boy, Shigeyuki, ought to be coming back soon. But then an official letter arrived, saying that he'd been killed in the war. He'd been killed in the Philippines round about the time that they'd dropped the atom bomb. His remains never came back. They just gave me a little slip of wood with 'The soul of the late Corporal Shigeyuki Matsumoto' written on it. They say that if you die as a soldier you become a god, so I've put the slip of wood on the Shintō shelf for the family gods. But I still feel that it might have been better to have put it on the Buddhist household altar . . .

My husband and my elder boy only came back in my dreams. We didn't have the ashes or remains of either of them. So we just had a quiet funeral and there's nothing buried in their grave. Nothing at all!

Doing my husband's share of the work too

I started to feel better after my younger boy, Toshio, got back. His coming back was like flowers suddenly blooming in the house. As soon as he got back, he started to help me with the farmwork. The Fujiokas next door gave us some nightsoil, saying: 'If you don't have any fertiliser, you can't farm properly.'

Then Toshio started to go on the ox-cart to collect nightsoil. That ox knew that its owner was a woman, so it often used to play me up and behave wildly. While I was working in the fields, it would break through the wooden gate and damage the neighbours' crops. The neighbours would catch it and bring it back. I'd apologise and get upset. For quite a while after they dropped the atom bomb, it was one upset after another.

Toshio was interested in electricity and, after a while, he started to say that he wanted to go out to work. Each day he'd go off to work in an electrical goods shop over towards Yokokawa, so I did the farmwork on my own. We had as much as 7 *tan* [about 1³/₄ acres], so I did my best to keep the land in good shape and at least to keep the weeds down. I wasn't bothered about growing good crops, but at least I didn't want to be laughed at as a farmer who grows weeds. Because our family was small, we had a big quota of sweet potatoes and barley to deliver up to the authorities. So it was just a case of growing and delivering, growing and delivering.

We don't have any paddy fields now. We've just got 3 *tan* [about ³/₄ acre] of dry land. Last year we levelled about 2 *tan* and built some flats. Toshio has been working for the Chūgoku Power Distribution Company for more than 30 years now. When he said that he wanted to build some flats, I agreed. You've got to face up to the fact that the world is changing.

Together with my daughter-in-law, I'm farming our 3 *tan* of dry land. I keep good health and I'm grateful that I can still work. It's a waste of time to just mooch around. I'm a farmer and working is my life. These days we grow cucumbers and aubergines all the year round, so I don't even manage to tend the grave. There are weeds growing round the grave and I haven't even changed the flowers. I'm so busy with the farmwork that I find myself going out into the fields all the time.

Up till now, I've never been ill even once. Except when I had my babies, I've never lay in. I think it's rather strange that I've never even had any rheumatism. I suppose I must have been blessed with

my husband's share of good health as well as my own. As long as
you work, you can keep up your strength.

Yet even though I keep good health and can still work, I still miss
my husband. Until quite recently, I used to long for him to come
back. But he won't come back now. It was after I turned 80 that at
long last I resigned myself to that. If he'd died from some ordinary
illness, I would have accepted it. But when I get to thinking that he
was burnt by the atom bomb and died that way, even now there are
nights when I can't sleep.

I talk to my grandchildren about the atom bomb, but however
much you talk to them, if they weren't actually there, they can't
understand how terrifying it was. You can talk to people who didn't
actually experience it, but they don't really understand when they
say: 'Oh! I see!' Still, I can't keep quiet about how terrifying it was,
so I tell them all the same. I've been thinking of leaving a written
record of how my husband was killed by the atom bomb, so I'm
pleased that you've come to see me.

Every morning I ask my husband, when I look at his photograph:
'Keep me fit, and able to work, today as well.'

Then I chant a sutra. At night, when work is over, I look at his
photograph with a feeling of gratitude. But all the same, not every
day is a good day. There have been many days when even looking at
his photograph hasn't eased my heart . . .

In this village we all met the same fate at the same time. We've
lived on by comforting one another. There are things which on your
own you couldn't endure but, being together, we've lived through
them. But things like atom bombs should never be allowed. If only
for the sake of the generations of children to come . . .

17   Toshiko Yokochi

17 The Death of My Husband and Two Children
Toshiko Yokochi

We carried him on a door

The atom bomb was terrifying. I wish that in other countries too they weren't making things like atom bombs. If you drop an atom bomb, it's not just the soldiers, but lots of ordinary people too who get killed . . . The people who were killed by the atom bomb lived at a time when things were really in short supply. I think they'd be pleased if they could see how plentiful things have become in the world today.

Ever since the atom bomb was dropped, I've been in good health and kept on working. I suppose it's because I keep working that my health is good. Most of the time I work hard, but I look forward to going to the hot springs at Yunotsu (in Shimane Prefecture) four or five times a year. Almost every January, I go with Haru Takasaki and the others to the hot springs at Beppu (in Ōita Prefecture).

I didn't have any brothers, so I inherited my parents' land. I was born on 1 December 1906. I must be 75 now. I had one younger sister, but she died in a road accident 27 years ago (in 1954).

After finishing Kawauchi Higher Elementary School, I helped with the farmwork at home. We had 7 *tan* [about 1³/₄ acres] of dry land and 3 *tan* [about ³/₄ acre] of paddy fields. So by those days' standards, we had a big farm.

On 21 October 1926, I had an arranged marriage with a man from a farming family in the same village, called Magoichi. I remember it well because the Taishō Emperor died in December of the same year that we were married. My husband was four years older than me. He'd been born in 1903. He liked to drink and was a rough and manly type. He was in the Reservists' Association and used to train the others in bamboo-spear drill.

143

For a time before they dropped the atom bomb, he was an official in the Volunteer Guards. He was very busy, rushing about here and there, helping with things.

On the morning of the 6th, he set off as usual without saying anything special. On 4, 5 and 6 August, for three days, he went off to Hiroshima to dismantle buildings, under the command of the Reservists' Association. He wasn't to know that he'd be killed by the atom bomb, so like I said, he went off without saying anything special.

In those days, we were growing a lot of millet. Together with my parents and my eldest boy (Hajime, 17 years old at that time), I'd gone to our field at Jōnan to thin out the millet. Just when I was thinking that the sun was getting high, there was a noise like a big BANG. It was a shock and I threw myself face down on the ground. When I raised my head to take a look, a white mass had risen into the sky over Hiroshima. Thinking that something terrible must have happened, I climbed up on to the embankment. Just then, I happened to notice that the Jōnan bamboo wood had been flattened, as if it had been steam-rollered. Then gradually the trees started to straighten up again. Over where Jōnan Middle School is now, it was all a bamboo wood in those days . . . Myself, I didn't notice any flash at the time, although everyone says that there was a blinding flash.

When I went back to look at the house, it was in a terrible state. The *shōji* screens were all askew, the ceiling had been pushed up, and a lot of soot had fallen down from the straw roof. I'd closed the doors when I went out, and that made the damage worse.

I had a lot of children. I'd brought up seven. My eldest boy, whom I mentioned before, was called Hajime. My second boy was called Shigemi and he was 15 at the time. My third boy was called Takaharu and he was 5. And my fourth boy was called Kazuyoshi; he was 2. As for the girls, my eldest was called Chizuko and she was 19. My second girl was Yōko and she was 11. And my third girl was Sakae; she was 8. Yōko and Sakae came back from elementary school crying their eyes out. I thought immediately that everybody who had gone to Hiroshima would probably have been hurt. My eldest girl, Chizuko, had been at home since leaving Gion Girls' Higher School, so together with my husband, she'd gone off with the Volunteer Corps. My second boy, Shigemi, was in the second year at Sōtoku Middle School. The first thing I thought was what could have happened to my children and husband . . .

I was so worried that I couldn't keep still, and kept on popping in and out of our damaged house. Old Man Shimonaka (the next-door neighbour) told me:

'Everybody from Kawauchi seems to have been hurt.'

I couldn't bear waiting any longer. Thinking that Shigemi might be on his way back, I went as far as Higashihara in Gion to meet him. A lot of injured people were making their way back. People were saying:

'Things are terrible in Hiroshima. Don't go there! Don't go!'

So against my will, I turned back and returned home to wait.

As the sun was going down, somebody said that the people from Kawauchi would be coming back by boat. Thinking that my husband might come back, Hajime and I took one of the sliding doors out of its grooves and went to meet him at Nakachōshi, on the bank of the River Ōta. When I got there, I found that my husband was among those on the boat and that he was still alive. Although people had told him not to drink, he was scooping water out of the river with a bucket and drinking it. His face and body were so swollen with burns that his eyelids were turned inside out. The skin had peeled off his hands and was hanging down. All he was wearing were his pants. His vest and trousers had been burnt, so he was all but naked. He didn't have his *chikatabi* plimsolls on either. All that was left of his hair was the part that had been covered by the hat he was wearing. The rest had all been burnt.

I suppose it was because he was burnt and his body had swollen up that he was so heavy. We put him on the door, and with Hajime in front and me behind, we started to carry him. But he was so heavy that we had to put him down and rest at the Shinmura Shop. On the door, my husband kept on groaning 'Water! Water!' He was an awful weight and as we carried him home I was wondering if he could be saved with such terrible burns.

Tending my dying husband

I cleared up the mess in the house and put my husband on a mattress, but I didn't have any idea what would be the best way to look after him. Again and again, he asked me for water:

'I want a drink of water! Won't you give me some water?'

But people said that if I gave him water, he'd die. So I boiled up some thin rice gruel and gave him that to sip. He kept on worrying about the children. He'd say:

'I suppose Chizuko has been hurt too . . .

'I wonder what's become of Shigemi . . .'

And all the time he was worrying about Chizuko and Shigemi, he'd keep on begging:

'I want some water! Won't you give me some water?'

While all this was going on, one of the villagers came and told me:

'Your Chizuko has been brought back by boat to Ōshiba. From there, they're going to take her to Yutani in Gion. So please go there to collect her.'

I can't remember for the life of me who it was who came to tell me, or what his name was.

Although I'd been told that Chizuko was alive and had taken refuge at Yutani, I couldn't go to her because I had to look after my husband. I stayed by my husband's side, but all the time I was praying that Chizuko could hold on. When evening came on, my husband started to say:

'I've got a pain in my belly. Haven't we got any medicine?'

I gave him some medicine that we happened to have in the house, but it didn't help at all.

From the middle of the night, my husband stopped asking so often for water. He said to me:

'I've had it! Please bring up the children properly.'

With his swollen eyes and turned-back eyelids, he didn't seem able to see me any more. He was waving his burnt and skinned hands in the air. I said:

'Please keep up your strength. Please dear, you must hold on for the children's sake . . .'

But he said: 'I've had it!'

They were his last words. I kept on crying 'Dear! Dear!', but he'd gone. With burns like his, he couldn't have been saved.

Our five remaining children – our eldest boy Hajime, Yōko, Sakae, Takaharu and Kazuyoshi – were at my side. Together with them, I dabbed water on my dead husband's lips – those swollen lips which had kept on gasping for water. The house was so shaken up that the sliding doors wouldn't fit into their grooves any more and all we could do was prop them up. In that rickety house, I hung up a big mosquito net and sat up inside it all night, together with my children and my husband's dead body.

It was only later that I got to thinking that although my husband had been burnt, at least he got back alive and we had a chance to talk. In many other houses, there was no body and not even a trace of their loved ones. But I brought my husband home, nursed him, and was with him when he died. I count myself lucky.

Even though my husband had died, I couldn't afford to cry. Now I started worrying about Chizuko and Shigemi, neither of whom had got back. I thought to myself that I must go to Chizuko.

I found my daughter wearing only a pair of knickers

Early on the morning of the 7th, I told my dead husband:

'I know you might be lonely, but I'm going to get Chizuko, so please lie there quietly.'

But, of course, he was dead, so there was no reply . . . His face looked just as though he was sleeping peacefully. I told Hajime to look after the children and, pulling the handcart, I hurried to Yutani. Yutani Factory was full of dead and injured. Some were groaning and others were asking for water. Near to the entrance, Kiyoto Nomura was still alive. He was burnt terribly and was almost naked. He said:

'I want to drink some water. Could you bring me some?'

I said: 'I'll bring you some in a minute.'

He said: 'Chizu was lying down at the far end of this warehouse. She's burnt terribly, so even if you see her face, you won't know it's her. So you'd better call out her name.'

Mr Nomura was still completely conscious.

Calling out 'Chizuko! Chizuko!' in a loud voice, and pushing my way through the injured, I reached the far end. Then I heard Chizuko's voice, saying:

'Mum! Over here!'

'Is it you, my little Chizu . . . ?'

In the dim light of the warehouse, it was a living hell. It was there that I found Chizuko.

The first thing Chizuko said was:

'Have Dad and Shigemi got back home?'

I couldn't tell her that her father had got back last night and then died at home. I told her:

'Dad's been burnt, but he got back home safely. We haven't heard anything about Shigemi yet, though . . .'

Chizuko said: 'Oh! That's good.'

Her blouse and *monpe* trousers must have been burnt. All that was left was the elastic waist of her *monpe* trousers stuck to her body. Only her knickers were in one piece. Apart from that, she didn't have a stitch on her body. She was the sort of girl who always kept her hair neat, but now it was all anyhow. Her face was swollen with burns and she was so disfigured that I wouldn't have known it was Chizuko if it hadn't been for her voice.

She said: 'Mum, I want a drink of water.'

There was a noodle bowl nearby, so I went and got some warm water in it and gave it to Chizuko to drink. She drank it all as though it tasted delicious. After a while, she said:

'Mum, I want to go to the lav.'

But she no longer had the strength to stand up. Holding my hand, she uttered her last word: 'Mum!' Without ever going to the lav, she breathed her last. I think it must have been about 6.40 p.m. Our neighbour, Mr Tochimura, was there and he said:

'She's gone and there's nothing more we can do for her. Let's take her home.'

So we carried Chizuko outside.

Kiyoto Nomura, who'd told me where Chizuko was, was already dead, clinging to the fence by the entrance. When I'd arrived, he'd still been alive and he'd told me the place where I could find Chizuko. But now . . . He'd asked for a drink of water and I'd promised to bring him some later. But I hadn't known I'd be busy with Chizuko and, in the end, I never brought him any water. I felt really badly about it.

We took Chizuko home and laid her down beside her father. Neither of them would ever ask for a drink of water again. It broke my heart to look at them.

On the evening of the 7th, we took my husband and Chizuko to the place for burning the bodies and we cremated them together there. The children hardly said a word when, later that night, they helped me to pick up Chizuko's and their father's bones. Nobody else came – not even our relations or the neighbours. Everybody was in the same boat . . .

Grinding my husband's bones into powder

On the morning of the 8th, one of the villagers came to tell me:

'Shigemi is at Ōshiba Embankment. Please go and collect him.'

So pulling the handcart behind me, I now hurried to Ōshiba to fetch Shigemi. Shigemi was on the embankment with two of his classmates and they were still alive.

Shigemi told me that the bomb went off during roll-call at Fukuya Department Store, before they started work on dismantling houses.

He told me that everybody's back suddenly burst into flames, and that the backs of their jackets and trousers were instantly burnt up. He said that they beat out the flames for each other with their hands, but the skin on their backs was burnt terribly. Trying to escape from the fires, they made their way to Hiroshima Station and jumped into the river. Then they waited for the tide to go out and climbed up on to Ōshiba Embankment.

'I've brought the cart, so get on quickly,' I said to him, and got him on to the cart. He kept on complaining: 'It's hot, Mum. It's hot!' When I gave him the paper umbrella which I'd brought with me, he clutched it firmly in his burnt, sore hands and held it up for shade.

'I want a drink of water, Mum.'

Again and again he asked for water, and another thing he said was:

'We must tell the school, Mum. We must tell them that I'm going back home.'

I told him: 'The school's completely burnt down, so there's no way we can let them know. There's no need for you to worry. Mum will see to it later . . .'

But however much I told him, he still kept on, again and again: 'We must tell the school . . .'

When we got back as far as the bamboo wood at Gion, I put the cart in the shade and asked Shigemi if he'd like a rice ball. But he said that, more than a rice ball, he wanted water. In the wood, there was any number of black, charred bodies. They'd fled from Hiroshima and used their last drop of energy to get here, only to die. There were a lot of people who were still alive too. They kept on groaning and asking for water. Those groaning voices filled the whole wood and sounded like a dirge.

People who weren't there when the atom bomb was dropped say all sorts of things about the bomb. But unless you actually saw it, I don't think you can really understand how cruel it was . . . Somebody who fought in China said to me:

'In all the battles that I've been through, I've never seen such a horrible way of dying as this.'

Some time after mid-day, we eventually got back home and I laid him on a mattress. He babbled on and on:

'I was thinking that if I got on to the Ōshiba Embankment, you would come and get me, Mum . . . When I waded across the river, the water was above my waist . . . I lay down on the embankment. The town and Ushida Hill were on fire, and they did look pretty . . .

My legs were injured, so I couldn't walk any further. I saw people die in front of my eyes. I was waiting and hoped you'd come quickly, Mum.'

I listened to him, and kept on nodding and saying things like, 'Oh, did you . . . ?' My heart was breaking and I could hardly bear it.

He'd escaped with his bare life to Ōshiba Embankment, and there he'd spent the night, lying on the sand, seeing people dying and the injured fleeing, and watching the town and the hillside as they burned. When I thought about what he'd been through, it was heartbreaking. It made me so angry to think that a child in the second year of middle school should have had to go through that terrible experience. To nobody in particular, I screamed in my heart: 'What is this terrible thing you've done to my child . . . ?' Inside me, I was boiling with anger as I looked after Shigemi.

People said that powdered human bones were good for burns. So I got my husband's bones that we'd cremated the evening before (7 August) and ground them up in an earthenware mortar. Then I put the powdered bone on to Shigemi's burns. But it didn't work at all. My husband's bones had been poisoned (by the radiation from the atom bomb), so of course they wouldn't work. I realised that later . . . All the same, I was desperate enough at the time to try anything. But it's a nightmare to think that on that night I ground up his father's bones, my husband's bones, in an earthenware mortar and put the powder on my boy's burns.

Neither on the way home, nor after we'd got back home, did Shigemi say a word about his father or his elder sister, who were already dead. It's strange that he didn't ask about them. I wonder why . . . ? Since he was on the Ōshiba Embankment for more than one night, someone from the village might have told him about the death of his father and sister. Even so, you'd have thought he'd have asked about his father at least once. But he never asked about either of them. And I didn't say a word about them either.

Until he died, all he kept on saying, every now and again, was: 'We must tell the school . . .'

It was about 4 o'clock on the afternoon of the 8th that Shigemi breathed his last. Then we set about making the third coffin.

Seventeen-year-old Hajime helped me a lot. He was in the second year of the regular course at the Prefectural Technical School, but he gave up school in the middle of his studies and started to work on the farm for me. In those days, you couldn't grow crops unless you went and brought nightsoil from Hiroshima. Even though Hajime was still young, he used to take the horse and cart, and go to collect nightsoil.

Although I'd lost my husband and two children, I couldn't have cried even if I'd felt like crying. I didn't even feel lonely. All I could think about was the future – from now on, what would we do? Because of the state we were in, for a while we couldn't grow any good crops, although the weeds were certainly thriving. It was a time when food was in short supply, so I eked out the rice by adding *mouli* and potatoes to it, and brought up my growing children in that way.

Hajime was the eldest boy and he threw up school and sacrificed everything for me. Since then, Hajime has put his heart and soul into the farmwork. My daughter-in-law, Teruko, is a good person, too, and she manages the house really well.

After the war, we farmers lived from hand to mouth and we were really hard-up. These days, I often think that we did well to get through that period. Nowadays, whatever it is you want, there's almost too much of it, so it makes you realise just how hard things were after the war.

Even now, I can sometimes feel the weight of my dying husband as I carried him home with Hajime on that door. How he must have suffered when he was burnt by the atom bomb. I sometimes wonder whether that suffering of his turned into a weight. Was that perhaps why he was so heavy? It's the type of memory which only people who've had a really cruel experience can understand, and it's my karma to carry it with me till I die.

18 Kazu Shimooke

18 He's Never Far from My Thoughts

Kazu Shimooke

Helping my son, who is on his own

I was born on 5 July 1896 and I'll be 85 this year. . . . As usual, I got up at 5 o'clock this morning and went out to pick long aubergines. Up until a little while ago – about 8 o'clock – I was out in the rain, picking the aubergines, so that's why you'll have to excuse me for looking so mucky.

We've got 6 *tan* [about 1½ acres] of dry land and it's hard work to keep up with the farming. I'm the oldest person round here, but still I'm working. The reason why is that my daughter-in-law, Eizō's wife, died two years ago. So I have to do the work now, because if we employed somebody, we couldn't make ends meet. If I didn't work, we couldn't carry on and that would be hard on my son. Three years ago, I got a stomach ulcer. Over the next twelve months, I had an injection every two weeks and that cured me. Up to then, I'd never been under the doctor. Even my eyes are as sharp as ever. I can see really well. By the way, your hair's rather thin, isn't it? How old are you? . . . 58, you say. Oh, that's no age!

Since I'm getting on, I can't work as well as an able-bodied farmer, but I can still help my son a bit.

I was born on a farm near to the Bishamon Shrine in Iwaya. That was in the next village to this, called Midorii. We farmed about 1 *chō* [about 2½ acres] of paddy fields. My father was called Shūhei; my mother was called Tamayo; and I was the eldest of four children. I often used to look after my younger brothers.

After leaving Midorii Elementary School, I went to Gion Higher Elementary School. There were only about three of us from the village who went on to higher elementary school. I used to walk about 1 *ri* [about 4 kilometres] to school. As soon as I got back from school, I'd get on with the sewing or looking after the babies. In those days, we really had to help about the house. Even children at elementary school had to pull their weight.

I got married on 20 January 1913, not long after the New Year. I was 18 at the time. My husband's name was Isaku Shimooke. Out of eight children, he was the eldest boy. He was a quiet type and a good man. His family had about 7 *tan* [about 1³/₄ acres] of dry land, but not much paddy. In summer, we grew as much as 4 *tan* of hemp. We used to cut down trees on the hillside and use them as firewood when we steamed the hemp. Even now, I still keep the steaming baskets that we used in those days. It's mostly dry land round here, so all we had to eat was a horrible barley/rice mixture. For a while after coming here to get married, I found things really hard. I was surprised at how poor the food was, and we were busy working right through the year. Life was really hard in those days.

Midorii, where I came from, had a lot of paddy fields. I came here to get married thinking that life would be easy in a place where there was mainly dry land. But it was a disappointment to find that people even used to say about this place: 'Don't send your daughters to get married in Nukui or Nakachōshi!' All the same, my health has been good and I've been happy working here. I had eight kids as well.

If only they hadn't dropped the atom bomb, I suppose I'd be happy living out my last days with my husband. My husband was 60 when he was killed by the atom bomb, and I was 50. War is awful; it brings nothing but misery to people.

Searching among the dead bodies

My husband had seven brothers and sisters, but only two of his sisters are still alive now. I had eight kids, but one of them died early, so I brought up seven – five boys and two girls.

When they dropped the atom bomb, my eldest boy, Hayato, was 30. My second boy, Tadao, had been killed in the war two years earlier. My third boy, Eizō, was 24 and he'd gone to fight overseas. My fourth boy, Shirō, was 20 and he'd been called up too. My girls, Sachiko and Sachiyo, were 13-year-old twins. And my youngest, Rokurō, was 8. Does that make seven? Five of them are still alive now.

Including my husband's, I've got photographs of seven people lined up in a row on the lintel. No, wait a minute, it must be eight, because there's also the photograph of my daughter-in-law, who died not so long ago. Morning and night, when I pray in front of the household altar to the Buddha, they all look down on me kindly. I look up at the photographs and think to myself that they're all looking after me.

Now I'll tell you about the morning that my husband was killed by the atom bomb. My husband kindly said to me:

'We'll finish dismantling the houses today, so from tomorrow I'll be at home. We can do the work about the house tomorrow, so today everybody can forget about work and take it easy.'

Then he urged our daughter-in-law (the eldest son's wife) to go to see her parents for the day and enjoy herself. Those were my husband's parting words to me. He was always a kind person, but I wonder if human beings can feel that they're going to die? That morning my husband's voice sounded even kinder than usual. Even now, I can remember it well.

After seeing my husband off, I went to the nearby stream to do the washing. While I was doing the washing, there was a noise like a big BANG. I thought that a bomb might have fallen somewhere nearby, so instead of going back home, the Nagaos let me into their air-raid shelter. At the time, I was concerned more about saving my own skin than about my husband or children . . .

When I went back to the house to take a look, I found that a glass sliding door had been broken and that the clock was smashed. The blast wave must have got in through a sliding door that I'd left open. The wooden doors in the earth-floored porch had been sent flying, as though the Asura God had been breaking the place up.

Some time after mid-day on the 6th, the injured started to come back. I realised that something awful must have happened. My husband and my eldest boy didn't come back, and I was like a cat on hot bricks. My eldest boy's wife went off to search for them, and when she came back she told me that the whole town was a sea of fire, so that she'd only been able to get so far.

Early on the morning of the 7th, I set off with my other children to search for my husband and my eldest boy. Around Aioi Bridge and Motoyasu Bridge there were heaps of charred and cruelly burnt bodies. There were bodies everywhere – in the river, on the embankment . . . – and at one place there were a lot of dead pupils from the Hiroshima No. 1 Higher School for Girls, looking like goby fish being dried in the sun. They'd died sitting in a row on the steps of a pier. Strange to say, not one of those girls had died with her legs apart. Around the fire-brigade's water tanks, a lot of people had died with their heads dipping into the water. At Aioi Bridge, a soldier had died clinging to his horse, which had burnt to death. It was heartbreaking to see.

For four days, from the 7th to the 10th, we searched all over. As I walked along, I'd turn over each body to see its face, asking myself whether this could be my husband or my son. I didn't even think it was scary. My daughters complained that their feet hurt with so much walking, but I'd urge them on. We'd start walking again, turning over first one body and then another. Some bodies were covered with straw mats that we'd lift up to get a better look. Maggots were pouring out of their noses and mouths. White worms from the bodies' guts were crawling out of their mouths. All the faces were covered with burns and sores, so that they looked more like devils than people. You couldn't tell which person it was. Among them were some people who were still alive and they would beg us again and again for water. Harumi Sugita and me took sticks with us to turn over the bodies. Once or twice I'd peer down at a body and say to her:

'This one's a lot like your old man.'

For four days, we did all we could to find them. We took clothes and bandages in a bundle with us, but we couldn't find my husband or my son anywhere.

The empty grave

This village (Kawauchi Village) was named as the assembly point for people fleeing from Tōkaichi in Hiroshima. Tōkaichi was burnt down and the injured came streaming in. Kawauchi Elementary School was overflowing with people who'd been brought here on the Volunteer Guards' carts. As the days went by, they died one after another. Their bodies were lined up on the riverside and they were cremated there. Although I looked on from nearby, I didn't feel like helping the others. Even tears wouldn't come. My husband's and eldest boy's bodies hadn't been found and I could only think that after they'd been burnt, they'd jumped into the river and been carried away on the tide.

Like I said, for four days I walked all over, searching for them. I'd fill up a pop bottle with water at Mitaki and, taking a swig from that every now and again, I'd press on into the town. In the area around the Industrial Promotion Office (the epicentre of the atomic explosion) – it must have been about the 8th, I should think – there

were people who were still alive and begging for water. But I knew
that if I gave them any water, it would kill them, so I walked on
without giving them a drop. Besides, I couldn't be bothered with
other people's troubles.

From about the 10th, I started to have tummy trouble. By about
the 18th, I couldn't get up. They said it was dysentery and I was
taken to the Isolation Hospital in the village. So in the end, I couldn't
go out searching any more.

My sons were all in the army. So while I stayed in hospital, it was
just my eldest boy's wife, my twin daughters and my youngest boy
who were left at home. I couldn't eat a thing and at one stage I
couldn't even stand. I didn't know whether I was awake or whether
I was dreaming, but I had the illusion that I was wandering through
the smouldering wastes of Hiroshima and that my burnt and blistered
husband was smiling at me. It must have been the water that I'd
been scooping into my pop bottle at Mitaki that had made me bad.
That awful dysentery left me really washed out. And when I was just
about getting over the dysentery, the floods came. Although I wanted
to leave the hospital, I was stuck there until the floods subsided.

Talking about floods, it was awful round here. East of us, there's
the main branch of the River Ōta, and to the west flows the River
Furu, so in heavy rain we had to worry about the threat both from
the west and from the east. Every summer, the floods would come
in early July. Since I came here to get married, the household altar
to the Buddha has been under water about four times. Once the
embankment at Shimo Nukui had been breached, it would turn into
a sea round here. Boats could pass right over the fields. When it
flooded, we'd bring big tubs into the rooms and put the *tatami* mats
on top of them. The flood on 17 September 1945 (the Makurazaki
Typhoon) was terrible.

The floods went down and when I was ready to leave the hospital,
it was a really nice surprise to see Shirō come to collect me with the
handcart. He'd just been demobbed. It was an awful illness and when
I got back home, I really felt that there's nowhere like your own
place.

Even though I'd got over the dysentery, still my husband and son
hadn't come home. Since we didn't have their bodies, we couldn't
have a funeral. After about one month had passed, my twin daughters
and I started to lose our hair and we ended up completely bald.
Perhaps I shouldn't have taken the children with me when I went to
search for my husband and son. It was awful to look at my daughters'

bald heads because I couldn't help worrying that, if they'd lost all their hair, they might even die.

Even though I'd survived, for a while I didn't feel like working at all. I was still weak from the dysentery, but on top of that, what joy could there be in a house without a husband or eldest son? Strange to say, however thickly the weeds were growing in the fields, it didn't bother me at all for a while. Even now it plays on my mind, where my husband and eldest boy are, and what happened to them. However many years go by, the tears never dry.

We never had a funeral. You can't have a funeral for people when you don't know whether they're dead or alive. I didn't want to have one. But at least I did the right thing by attending the village funeral. Although we didn't have any ashes to put in the grave, they'd both smoked, so we buried a tobacco pouch that was left in the house. We had my husband's and eldest boy's names carved on the grave, but inside it was empty.

Working in the fields throughout the year

Even at the end of August, the potatoes were still in the ground. Our delivery quota for potatoes was 200 *kan* (about 750 kilogrammes). My husband had been called away so often to help with the construction of Kamine Airfield that he hadn't managed to deliver the potatoes. We were all behind with the work, so we had to pay people to dig up the potatoes for us. In the end, we never did deliver those potatoes, even though we had 200 *kan* of them packed up in straw bags.

When the autumn breeze started to blow, we needed fertiliser for the barley. With my husband dead, there was no one to collect nightsoil. It was an enormous job to look after 6 *tan* [about 1¹/₂ acres] of land. After my husband died, I don't know how we survived, but all I do know is that I was always working in the fields. And thanks to that, I kept my health.

My husband, Isaku, was 60 and my eldest boy, Hayato, was 30. Since the day it happened, it's as though they've both disappeared without trace. My father-in-law, Gonbei, died in 1926 when he was 74 and my mother-in-law, Nami, died in 1931 when she was 71. My second son, Tadao, was also killed in the war, in 1943. Anyway, like I said before, there are photographs of eight people who've passed away lined up in the best room. Morning and night, when I kneel in front of the Buddhist altar, I pray to those photographs as well. I look up at them and think to myself that they're all looking after me.

I worked hard, and Eizō really did well too. Take a look at that framed certificate. He got a prize for his Chinese leaves at the first Satō Township Agricultural Festival in 1958. He's a boy who's really put his heart into his farming. Ever since he took over the farm from his father, he's worked steadily. Up until recently, he was Director of the Satō Agricultural Cooperative.

But then, after all we'd been through, he lost his wife. She died on 27 December the year before last. It was cancer. There's no cure for an illness like that and now it's sad to see Eizō all on his own. I'm 85, but I was up at 5 o'clock this morning, helping him in the fields. We never let the land lie idle. Throughout the year, we've got something in the ground – 3 *tan* [about ³/₄ acre] of cauliflowers or cabbages, 2 *tan* [about ¹/₂ acre] of aubergines and 8 *se* [just under ¹/₄ acre] of lettuces. Eizō's only got an old woman like me to help him. Now that his wife's not with us any more, I can't afford to die.

I hate weeds. No matter whether the weather's hot or cold, I'm out weeding. In the days after my husband passed away too, the only relief I could get was to go out weeding. I can't stand weeds and I suppose that doing the weeding somehow helps to ease the feeling of missing my husband.

Anyway, as you've seen, everywhere round here boards have been put up, saying 'Oppose the Sanyō Motorway!' If that motorway gets built, it will destroy houses like mine that are more than 100 years old, the fields and everything. Sooner or later, I'll have to move the family graves, including my husband's. It really upsets me to hear them talking about destroying our farms. Soon there'll be no more farming. I don't want their money. If we could make just enough to live on as farmers, I'd be satisfied. But it's a sign of the times, I suppose, so I've more or less given up hope.

Since 1956, I've gone to Beppu every year with the Widows' Association. Haru Takasaki, who's organised the Association for many years, said to me:

'Let's go to Beppu again in the New Year.'

But what with my daughter-in-law dying and us being so busy, I've decided not to go. Every year, we say to each other:

'This year might be our last, so let's go to the hot springs at Beppu.'

But it wouldn't be fair to Eizō if I went to Beppu and wasn't here to help him with the farmwork. So I've decided not to go for the time being. And in the meantime, I might get an invitation to go and join my husband, rather than an invitation to Beppu!

Every evening, I chant a sutra in front of the Buddhist altar. And when I'm doing it, I can see Dad's (her husband's) face. He's never far from my thoughts.

19   Chiyoko Sugita

19 Bringing Back My Dead Husband
Chiyoko Sugita

No time for New Year celebrations or festivals

Thank you for coming! What have I done to deserve to be as busy as this? It's been raining since morning, hasn't it? But even so, I've been outside weeding. I only stopped just now when the rain came on hard. Anyway, it's worked out well, your turning up now. Excuse my dirty feet and hands, but would you mind if we talked in the entrance porch?

I was born on 15 August 1904. I'll be 77 this year. My parents' house was in a place called Yamamoto, in Gion, in Asa District. They weren't farmers but were in the *tatami* matting business, so I'd never done any farmwork.

My husband was called Shigeru and he was born on 20 October 1896. That made him nine years older than me. He was a good, kind man. He was never sarcastic and we never had a single quarrel.

I married him on 11 November 1925. We had 3 *tan* 6 *se* [just under 1 acre] of paddy fields and 2 *tan* 8 *se* [about ³/₄ acre] of dry land. We used to grow onions, Kyō greens and millet. We grew about 2 *tan* of onions and when we brought them in, we'd raise the *tatami* matting and spread them on the wooden floor. I suppose we must also have grown about 1 *tan* of millet. After taking the grain, the rest of the plant we used for compost and for burning. We grew hemp as well. They used to say: 'Don't send your daughter to get married in a place where they grow hemp!' From time to time, we raised silkworms, or bought rushes and then wove them into mats. So we were always busy with the farmwork . . . Still, I was young in those days and could keep up with the work. I had one baby after another, so if we hadn't worked hard, there wouldn't have been enough food to go round.

I must tell you about collecting nightsoil. We used to go down to Hiroshima by boat, on the tide, to collect nightsoil. It was easiest to go to collect nightsoil on the ebbing tide, so even if it was 2 o'clock in the morning, we'd get up for the full tide. We used to pack up food for breakfast and for our mid-day meal in a big rice tub, like a barrel, and then set off. We'd gone halves with another family to buy the boat that we used for collecting nightsoil. We'd moor the boat to the embankment of the River Motoyasu in Hiroshima, and then we'd carry the nightsoil from town on poles and load it on to the boat. Then we'd wait for the rising tide under the Aioi Bridge. No matter whether it was a wet day or a windy day, we still couldn't put off going to collect nightsoil. My husband used to say:

'With a plump body like yours, you can work well!'

At the beginning of the Shōwa Era [late 1920s], you could get two types of tub for collecting nightsoil. One cost ¥1 and the other ¥1.50. The ¥1.50 type was made out of reddish cedar wood, and however often you washed it, it didn't wear out. It cost ¥15 to buy ten of those tubs. Sometimes we'd borrow the money off my parents to buy some tubs. Four or five years before the war broke out, we bought a Korean Red ox for ¥15 and switched to collecting the nightsoil by cart.

In 1931, my father-in-law had a stroke when he was earthing up the barley. Since my mother-in-law died on 19 January 1932, I had to look after my father-in-law after that. Until he died on 12 October 1936, I had to feed him by spoon at every meal. There was the farmwork to be done, the sick to be cared for, and the children to bring up. So what with one thing and another, I never had any time for New Year celebrations or festivals. For well nigh ten years, I never stepped outside the gate of the yard.

My husband often used to say to me:

'I'm really sorry, dear, that you can't visit your parents even at New Year or for the festival.'

But thinking that that was my fate, I just got on with whatever had to be done. Luckily, I was fit and well. And whenever my husband apologised, I'd just tell him not to worry about it.

Egg-roll and white rice in his lunch box

My husband was called up into the Hiroshima 5th Division as a first-grade conscript and became a private first class. He was put in the first reserve for six months and then in the second reserve for a further two months. After that, he went back to farming.

It wasn't only men who were mobilised for dismantling buildings in Hiroshima, but even women who didn't have young children to look after. I was still only 40, and my youngest boy was 7 and no longer any trouble, so I wanted to go with my husband.

It was decided that they'd be dismantling buildings from 4 August, so my husband and I finished delivering our barley quota to the authorities on the 3rd. I was quite prepared to be mobilised myself from the 4th, but then Hayato Shimooke (Kazu Shimooke's eldest son), who was an official of the neighbourhood association, came to see me and said:

'You needn't go. It will be tough in this heat, so don't you go.'

As it happened, then, I was working at home on the 4th and the 5th, although I still wished that I'd been sent to dismantle buildings. I wanted to go because I didn't want to be called a traitor. On the morning of the 6th, I said to my husband:

'I want to go too.'

But he said: 'Don't go. Don't go. You weed the lower paddy field.'

I don't know why I did it, but on the morning of the 6th I decided to put an egg-roll in my husband's lunchbox with his rice. I put some charcoal in a clay stove to cook the egg-roll. As I was cooking it, my husband passed by and patted my bottom, saying:

'Egg-roll today? What a treat!'

When I handed over the water flask and his lunch box, I said to him:

'Today you've got egg-roll and white rice, so you'd better hide it from the others when you eat!'

But as it turned out, my husband couldn't have eaten the food that I made for him. Even now, I can't understand why I packed him up an egg-roll and white rice on that particular morning. I've still got the clay stove that I used that morning for cooking the egg-roll. I can't help remembering my husband whenever I see that clay stove. He said:

'Today we've got just one house to dismantle. I'll be home early and, on the way home, I'll get the *tōfu* [bean curd] that I ordered yesterday.'

The day before, he'd taken 1 *shō* [about 1.8 litres] of soya beans to Kawamoto's *tōfu* shop in Midorii and left them to be turned into *tōfu*. On the day the atom bomb was dropped, he was planning to get home just after mid-day. He went off wearing khaki-coloured trousers with puttees. He'd got a hand towel hanging from his belt and a straw hat on his head. Even in my wildest dreams, I never thought that would be the last time I'd see him alive.

As soon as I'd seen off my husband, I went to the paddy field behind the elementary school, carrying the weeder over my shoulder. The sun had risen high in the sky and as I was pushing the weeder, I was thinking to myself that my husband and the other people from the village must be hard at work, dismantling buildings. Just then a big BANG seemed to come from the bottom of the world. Something seemed to swish by me and for a second my face felt warm. I was startled and looked round. I thought that a bomb might have dropped on the elementary school, so I put the weeder over my shoulder and hurried back home. The matting in the room had been turned upside down. I went next door and while we were asking each other what on earth could have happened, a B29 flew over again. We quickly dashed into the air-raid shelter.

When we came out of the shelter to take a look a little bit later, a cloud like an enormous ball was rising into the sky over Hiroshima. The neighbours had come out too and were scurrying about in all directions. I can't describe the feeling of uneasiness that built up inside me. I couldn't stay still, thinking to myself:

'I wonder if that's where Dad is? I think I'll go to see how things are at Kawamoto's (the *tōfu* shop) in Midorii . . .'

About 11 o'clock, people started to come back, saying that they'd been bombed in Yokokawa and Shinjō. They were making their way to the clinic at Midorii. I thought to myself that there was no point standing in front of Kawamoto's shop, watching the injured. Taking the *tōfu*, I had got back as far as Hironaka's shop (in Nukui) when one of the villagers called out to me from behind to stop. He told me: 'Shigeru may have been killed by a bomb.'

I threw the *tōfu* aside and rushed into the village office. An assistant was there, so I asked:

'Is it just my husband who's been hit by a bomb?'

He said to me: 'There's no official word that any member of the Volunteer Corps has been killed, so please remain calm. I'll let you know as soon as I get any information.'

But how could I remain calm when my husband's life hung in the balance? That was how things stood round about mid-day on the 6th.

My husband was rescued by boat

About mid-day, a notice from the village office was brought round. It said:

Those who have got boats should take them to pick up people from this village. It is impossible to go there on foot, because the roads are choked with people who have suffered burns. So please go by boat.

I couldn't stay at home. I went with the others to the landing place at the riverside. About 2 o'clock, a person from Kami Nukui came back by boat. He said:

'Everybody in the Volunteer Corps has had it. It looks as though the bomb fell right where the Volunteer Corps was.'

When I heard him say that, my legs started to tremble. Up until then, I'd been thinking that my husband was probably safe, but now it was as though a cold hand had touched my heart. Alongside me, there was Harumi Nagao, Kazu Shimooke, Sato Sugita and Toyono Wataru. All of our husbands had gone off with the Volunteer Corps, so we were all worried sick. Although they'd said that the Volunteer Corps 'had had it' or been 'wiped out', these were nothing more than rumours. Nobody knew for certain. It was frustrating, but all we could do was stand at the riverside, worrying.

About 6 o'clock in the evening, word came that Hayato Shimooke had been seen sitting on the steps of the Industrial Promotion Office. I ran to Kazu Shimooke's place and told her:

'They say your son's been found. Go quickly, and take some rice balls.'

Later I heard that although she went there, she couldn't find any trace of him.

Many boats had gone from Kawauchi Village to rescue the injured. They told us that around Aioi Bridge, the dead and injured were everywhere, both in the river itself and on the riverbank. Some of the injured clung to the sides of the boats, pleading 'Save me! Save me!' There were so many injured that those in the boats knew they couldn't help them all, so they told us that they asked the injured their names, and shouted:

'Is there anybody from Kawauchi?'

Then one person, who'd been burnt black, came up to the boat, saying:

'Please save me!'

'Who are you?'

'I'm Shigeru Sugita.'

'Shigeru, is it? Get on board quick!'

Two men in the boat pulled him on board, and it turned out to be my husband . . . The story I'm telling you now is the way I heard it from the boatmen later.

The boats coming upstream could only take three or four people on board. So they didn't come all the way back to Kawauchi, but put the injured on shore at Ōshiba. Then they went back to the River Motoyasu to pick up other Kawauchi people.

They told me that when they took my husband on board, he was asking for a drink of water. When they put him ashore at Ōshiba Embankment, he thrust his whole face into the river and drank a lot of water. They told him:

'Lie down here. We'll come back and get you later. All right?'

Nodding his head, he said: 'Thanks!' My husband was certainly still alive when they put him down at Ōshiba.

Night came on the 6th, and I was so worried and frustrated I didn't know what to do with myself. My supper just stuck in my throat. Outside, the night was dark and then I heard footsteps and one of the villagers came in. She told me:

'Shigeru's got back as far as Ōshiba. Go quickly to him!'

With one of the neighbours, I ran to Ōshiba.

There were lots of people on the embankment at Ōshiba. The darkness was alive with the sounds of groaning voices and people asking for water. As I searched for my husband, I was thinking to myself: 'If he's still alive, will he be sitting down somewhere, or will he be on his feet?' But I couldn't find him anyway. Even if he was there, with his body burnt black in that pitch darkness, there was no way that I could have known it was him.

There was nothing for it but to return home along the dark roads. On the way, I came across any number of injured, and passing in the opposite direction were other people going to search for their loved ones. When I got back home, one of the villagers told me:

'Your husband's passed away at Ōshiba and they've left him there for the time being. Tomorrow morning at about half past eight, you should go to Shōsō Temple at Minami Shimoyasu in Gion. They'll have taken his body there by then . . .'

I was so stunned that I couldn't make a sound, even to cry. Besides, it was no time for crying. I thought to myself: 'What's going to become of us? I must be strong . . .'

I knew it was my husband by his feet

It must have been about 9 o'clock on the morning of the 7th when I set out with the cart to collect my husband's body. I took my two eldest kids along with me.

Before going on, I'd better tell you about my kids. My eldest boy, Kazuo, died young, when he was still in the second year of elementary school. It was 9 May 1933. When my husband was killed, my second boy, Hideo, was 19. My eldest girl, Nobuko, was 17. My third boy, Masanobu, was 15. My second girl, Fumiko, was 13. My fourth boy, Yoshinobu, was 11. My third girl, Michiko, was 9. And my fifth boy, Shigenobu, was 7. So I brought up eight kids altogether.

If we'd been well off, and if my husband's parents had been fit and well, we could have lived comfortably. But on top of being poor, we had lots of kids too, so our life was really hard and you could say that my husband and I each had to do the work of two people. Even now, I can't forget how hard life was, working with my husband. And then, when he was killed by the atom bomb, I felt like a crab that has had its pincers snapped off!

Taking Hideo and Nobuko with me, I hurried to the Shōsō Temple in Gion, clutching the handle of the cart as I went. None of our relations or neighbours came with us. How could they? In every house, somebody had been burnt to death or was missing. In some houses, it was the husband; in others, the wife or the children. So no one could afford to look after other people. When we got to the temple, there were many, many bodies laid out in rows. Some were charred black and others were covered in burns and blisters. There must have been dozens, and even hundreds, of them. All the way down the drive leading up to the temple, and in the temple garden itself, there were so many bodies laid out that you could hardly pick your way between them. Their faces were covered with straw mats.

When we got on to the drive, I suddenly shouted, without thinking: 'This one is Dad!'

The second body in the right-hand line of corpses on the driveway was Dad. They'd laid him down there and covered him with a thin straw mat. I lifted the straw mat and saw Dad lying there, dead and gone for ever. All I could say as I cradled his head in my arms was:

'Oh my dear, what have they done to you?'

His body was charred, and it was so red and swollen that he looked like a skinned sparrow. But his face hadn't been burnt, and it looked peaceful in death.

One of the villagers said to me:

'Mrs Sugita, how did you know that was your husband, when all you saw were his feet?'

I said: 'We've lived together as man and wife for a good twenty years, so of course I knew it was my husband as soon as I saw his feet.'

And she said: 'Even so, you did well to find him straightaway among all these bodies.'

They all gathered round in amazement, seeing that I'd recognised my husband just by his feet.

My husband's feet had high arches. All that was left of the puttees that he'd gone out wearing that morning were the bits round his ankles, because it was there that they'd been wrapped round three times. A lot of sand had collected there. The upper part of the puttees was missing and must have been burnt away. Another thing that was still in place was the hand-made box, made out of Paulownia wood, on the belt round his waist. He'd used it for keeping his tobacco in.

We spread the mattress that we'd brought with us on to the cart, laid my husband on it, and covered his body with a straw mat. When we brought him out of the temple, the injured were still walking in an endless stream along the road. People had put the dead bodies of their loved ones on to handcarts and bicycle carts, and everyone was hurrying northwards. Fearing that there might be an air raid by American B29s, everybody avoided the main roads. For the same reason, we climbed on to the Ōshiba Embankment and rattled along its stony path. There were bamboo thickets and pine trees growing alongside the back roads, so we thought that there'd be places for us to hide whenever we were attacked by enemy planes.

The house had been damaged by the blast wave from the atom bomb, so we cleared up the mess and laid my husband's body in the best room. In the evening, my father popped in, and said:

'I just came to see you because I wondered how you were getting on.'

He didn't stay long, but even now I still feel grateful to him for coming at a time when his own grandson had been killed. Apart from him, nobody at all called by. There were just me and the children at my husband's wake.

We sat round my husband's body under a dim lamp (because of

the air-raid precautions). I tried to comfort my children and told them that I'd need them to help me now:

'However much we call out "Dad," he can't come back to us. You'll all have to work alongside me now and help your Mum.'

What else was there for me to say? All seven of my children sat with me with their hands together in prayer. Now and again, Nobuko and Fumiko would cry out 'Dad! Dad!' and cling to their father's dead body, as though they had suddenly realised what had happened.

We cremated my husband on the riverside

On the 8th, we had to cremate my husband, but we had no coffin. We didn't even have any wood in our house that we could use for making a coffin. So we went to the Kawauchi Agricultural Association to get some wood, and then the children and I knocked together a rough coffin in the yard. We didn't bother to plane the wood or anything like that. It was a really home-made effort.

We put a few flowers from the garden into his coffin. Then we loaded the coffin on to the cart and took it to the riverside round the back of the house. We couldn't use the village crematorium because there had been so many cremations there that it had been burnt out. That was why, from early morning, the villagers had been going to the riverside to cremate their loved ones.

When we got to the riverside, smoke was billowing up. All the way along, people were cremating their husbands, or their daughters, or their sons. We dug a hole in the shape of a human body and lined it with firewood. Then we put my husband's body on top and covered it with more firewood and straw. Then we began to cremate him. I'd never cremated anybody before, but I looked at the way the people nearby were going about it and arranged the firewood and straw as they did. I set fire to the straw and then all I could do was chant the name of the Buddha.

While I was cremating my husband, I looked around from time to time and saw that, one after another, people would come, dig a hole, and then start to cremate another body. The school had been used as a collecting point for some of the dead and injured. Dozens of times, they brought bodies in their coffins from there. Then they'd line them up, douse them in petrol, and cremate them. The smoke and smell of burning bodies filled the sky over the village in a pall of gloom. Later I thought to myself that if the ghosts of the victims of the atom bomb ever appear, it will be on the riverside at that spot.

I suppose it must have taken about two hours to cremate my husband. At first his head escaped the flames. We ought to have put more firewood round his head. In the end, we had to cremate him twice. I suppose that shows that my husband didn't want to die. As I burnt my husband's head, I was sobbing in my heart and telling him:

'How awful it must have been for you when you were burnt black and died. It's unbearable to be burnt just a little, but it must be hell to be burnt to death.'

I felt like sobbing at the top of my voice, but everybody was holding back their tears as they tended the fires that were cremating their loved ones.

We picked up my husband's bones and put them in a jar that we had in the kitchen. We didn't have anything like a proper box for putting his bones in. We went and asked the priest to come, but he couldn't manage to because there were funerals going on everywhere in the village. So the children and I chanted a sutra and gave my husband the best funeral we could. For the next two or three days, we spent most of the time in front of the household altar to the Buddha. Down by the riverside, they kept on cremating people for days. The injured people who'd been taken to the elementary school died one after another and then they disappeared into the sands of the riverside.

In this village, there were a lot of people who went off with the Volunteer Corps and never came back. Not even their bodies were found. It's true that my husband died, but at least we got his body back. I cremated my husband with my own hands and I count myself lucky for that.

All the same, there couldn't have been anything more terrible and cruel than what happened to us. There shouldn't be any wars. I often get students from women's junior colleges and the like coming to see me and asking me to tell them about the atom bomb. But I can't describe what I went through in ten or twenty minutes. So I've decided not to tell them anything. I can never forget the agony I went through when my husband was killed by the atom bomb, so all I say to them, over and over again, is:

'Make sure none of you ever gets caught up in any wars.'

My kids have all grown up and I've got grandchildren now. When my grandchildren call by from time to time, I tell them how terrifying the atom bomb was. But they don't listen. So I show them this book of photographs about Hiroshima. As long as they are photographs, my grandchildren will look at them. I've shown them this book any number of times, which is why the cover and inside pages are so dog-eared.

Collecting nightsoil with my children

The village women went off day after day to search for their husbands. But in my case, my husband's body had been brought back and I'd been able to cremate him myself. So I considered myself lucky. Those women who never found any trace of their husbands must have suffered much, much more than I did. I really felt sorry for them. In the end, after quite some time had passed, I started to feel like doing the farmwork again.

The crops in the fields don't wait for you just because your husband's died or because you're busy weeping. Without water and fertiliser, they soon start to wither. But we didn't have any fertiliser. So there was nothing for it but to go to Hiroshima and collect nightsoil. When I talked it over with the kids, one after another they said that they'd go with me. That was how I started to collect nightsoil, taking the kids along with me. I made Hideo give up working for Mitsubishi Shipbuilding.

I'd get up at 1 o'clock in the morning, boil up the rice, and at 2 o'clock we'd set off, after loading the tubs for collecting the nightsoil on to the horse and cart. Hiroshima had been almost completely flattened, but a few houses and shops in Kaniya (near the station) and Hijiyama had escaped. You can only get nightsoil where there are people, so that's where we had to go.

The houses where my husband had collected nightsoil when he was alive were around Kaniya. I thought that if I went from house to house, mentioning my husband's name, people who knew him might let me have some nightsoil . . . While I was walking round Kaniya, I happened to meet a man by the name of Shinoda, who'd originally come from Kawauchi Village. He was chairman of the neighbourhood association. I said to him:

'I wonder if I could get hold of some nightsoil round here? I'll bring vegetables and swap them for the nightsoil.'

He said: 'I should think everyone would be pleased to exchange nightsoil for vegetables. I'll tell my neighbours about it too.'

He was kind to us, and later on he told the people living in the railway company's houses about our offer.

When it came to actually having to scoop up the nightsoil, my sons couldn't stand it. So I did the scooping up, while my boys loaded the tubs on to the horse and cart. After they'd loaded about ten tubs, I'd leave the boys to take it home. I'd hurry back first, taking the rough path along the Ōshiba Embankment, and get straight on with the farmwork.

In winter, it was bitterly cold, going to collect nightsoil. Even with my old air-raid hood over my head, and wearing my thickest clothes, around 3 or 4 o'clock in the morning it would be perishing. Huddling behind the nightsoil tubs to get out of the wind, for the best part of two hours I'd be jolted about on that creaking horse and cart. We had to go twice a week to collect nightsoil.

Together with my kids, I was one of the first to start going to get nightsoil again, so we collected a lot of nightsoil in our cess pit. In fact, we collected more than we could use ourselves. Many of our neighbours needed nightsoil, but couldn't go to collect it themselves because they were short of hands. There were even some who had horses and carts, but couldn't use them because their husbands had died and they didn't know how to handle the horses. And it was too much for a woman to go 2 *ri* [about 8 kilometres] with a handcart to collect nightsoil. People came round, offering to plough up a field for us in return for some nightsoil, or asking if we'd sell them some of our nightsoil. We sold a cartload apiece to five or six houses, at ¥1.70 a time. There's nothing worse for a farmer than not having any nightsoil. So they were pleased to get ours.

When we went to collect nightsoil, we'd load up vegetables on the cart and hand them over to Mr Shinoda to distribute. The kids were very keen on collecting nightsoil and the neighbours all said how lucky I was. I'd often say to my kids:

'If Dad was still here, you wouldn't have to work as hard as this.'

During the war, the kids had been either called up into the army or had gone away with the Volunteer Corps, so they hadn't done much farming and weren't very good at it. All the same, I was determined to keep our 4 *tan* 5 *se* [just over 1 acre] of land in good shape and to give my kids a good upbringing. So rain or shine, I'd be out in the fields. If you don't put your back into it, you can't get through the work.

Since my husband died, I haven't been sick once. My husband must have been watching over me. Anyway, that's what I believed, and it gave me the strength to work and to put my all into the farming. The kids often tell me not to overdo it, but in fact I do work harder than I should do – and they know it.

Hideo is poorly and attending the hospital now. Yoshinobu's in-laws didn't have any sons, so when he married a girl from Minuchi, in Yuki (Saeki District), he was adopted into her family. Masanobu died in 1958. It's just Hideo's wife and me who do the farming now.

I always tell my kids: 'Dad is alive in your Mum's heart.'

I still work as hard as anybody. What kept me going was the thought that I had to keep working until I'd given all my kids a good upbringing. I'm 77 this year, so I've reached the age when I should be having my *ki no ji* old-age celebration. But I'm not going to have one. Throughout my whole life, I've never had a moment for myself.

You've listened to what I've been telling you really patiently. Come again any time. I'll be expecting you . . .

Editor's Afterword

Interrupting their prayers

Now that they have seen 30 seasons come and go, the trees in the Hiroshima Peace Memorial Park have spread their branches. Last year [1981], on the morning of 6 August, I walked through the park from east to west, threading my way between the trees. I was on my way to take part in the joint memorial service at the monument to the Kawauchi Nukui Volunteer Corps, which has been erected on the embankment of the River Ōta. Gathered there were the widows and bereaved families from Nukui, the community which experienced the full horror of atomic war. The widows are all old ladies now. Accompanied by daughters-in-law and grandchildren, they all came with bunches of flowers, which they had grown in their own gardens, clutched in their arms. Soon the space in front of the monument was covered in flowers and offerings to the dead, while incense wreathed around the monument and floated away into the sky above the river.

About 200 people from Nukui were gathered around the monument. At 8.15 sirens rang across the entire city. Everyone was deep in prayer. Fresh in their minds, as though it were only yesterday, were the memories of how those near and dear to them had been killed by the atom bomb. Thirty-six years ago, at 8.15, the Nukui Volunteer Corps was annihilated. Some came back to die, but many went missing without trace. Now their widows were quietly wiping away the tears with wrinkled hands.

The monument to the Volunteer Corps was erected on 6 August 1964, at a cost of ¥400 000 to the bereaved families. It is a sizeable monument, some 2 metres high and 3 metres across, and on the back of it are carved the names of those killed by the atom bomb. When you count them, there are 180 in all – 84 from Kami Nukui, 46 from Naka Nukui and 50 from Shimo Nukui. Of those 180, 94 were men and 86 were women. To the right of the monument is a memorial stone, on which is carved the following explanation, in the joint name of all the bereaved families:

Respectfully Offered to the Spirits of the Volunteer Corps Members

We shall never forget the scene of disaster and unspeakable sadness

176

which occurred at 8.15 a.m. on 6 August 1945. Here the atomic bomb was dropped and our beloved relatives suffered agonies in the veriest hell. Now they sleep here. By the authoritative order of the Army, one hundred and seventy-four* individuals made the supreme sacrifice. On the day in question, from early in the morning, they were engaged in the work of dismantling houses. They were members of the Kawauchi Volunteer Corps and were resident in the former Nukui Hamlets, which jointly constituted Kawauchi Village, in Asa District. It is unnecessary to mention here our detestation of the ravages of war, but suffice it to say that we bereaved families are still experiencing endless and heart-rending grief over our dear departed, who offered up their young lives. As a permanent testimony to their supreme sacrifice, and as a prayer that ye, O Spirits, may for ever be in peace, we, the bereaved families, have jointly consulted and decided to erect this monument at this time when signs of peace are emerging on earth.

The people of Nukui do not take part in the 'Memorial Service for the Victims of the Atom Bomb and Joint Peace Ceremony', which is sponsored by Hiroshima City Council. Instead, they pray at the monument to the Volunteer Corps, which they erected by their own efforts. The way the Nukui widows feel about this was well expressed by Haru Takasaki as follows:

'At the Peace Ceremony, the police turn out and control the crowds, and that's not what we understand by peace. We want to quietly pray for the souls of the departed, not take part in a ceremony where crowds gather and there's uproar. It's like a fairground.'

Last year, Prime Minister Zenkō Suzuki attended the Peace Ceremony in Hiroshima, to mark the 36th anniversary of the atomic bombing. He was the third Prime Minister to attend the Peace Ceremony, although it was five years since the previous visit by a Prime Minister. Standing in front of the Memorial Monument to the Atom Bomb, Prime Minister Suzuki vowed to uphold the three non-nuclear principles and to promote world peace. Immediately following this, the Prime Minister left the ceremony and, as a result, the joint memorial service at the monument to the Volunteer Corps was

---

* The difference between this figure and the above-mentioned 180 arises from the fact that six additional names were discovered and added to those on the monument, but the inscription on the memorial stone was not changed. [Translator]

interrupted. The riot police gave orders to halt the service and clear the road immediately because the Prime Minister's car was coming. The arrogant riot police issued their instructions, and the people from Nukui had to withdraw to the pavement and to the sides of their monument. People were grumbling:

'Why does he drive by here? He should get out and walk.'

Eventually, the Prime Minister went by without a single person waving a hand.

Ten metres away from the monument to the Volunteer Corps, there are two monuments, side by side, to the 352 staff and pupils of Hiroshima No. 2 Middle School and to the 270 pupils of Hiroshima Commercial School. Around each of these monuments too, they were in the middle of holding Buddhist memorial services. I wonder if the Prime Minister could understand from the look in the eyes of the people lining both sides of the road that it was he who had interrupted their prayers and forced them to clear a path for his car.

After the Prime Minister's car had passed by and the unbreachable line of riot police had withdrawn, the participants again gathered in front of the monuments. Then the services continued, with young Hiroshi Isenobō, representing the pupils of Hiroshima Municipal Jōnan Middle School (in Satō), vowing 'We shall go on to build a world of peace', and the bereaved families burning their incense. Up above, the white oleander blossoms brightened the overcast sky.

Like a pilgrim

On 10 November 1981, after completing all the interviews with the 19 atom-bomb widows, I walked all the way to Nukui from the monument to the Volunteer Corps. It is 12 kilometres as far as Kami Nukui. The old path climbs up on to Ōshiba Embankment, and then passes by Gion Ōhashi, Furuichi and Higashihara, before reaching Shimo Nukui. This is the path that the Nukui widows walked repeatedly when they went to Hiroshima to search for their husbands and children. Between Higashihara and Nukui, bamboo thickets are dotted about nowadays but, at the time when the atom bomb was dropped, there were bamboo thickets all the way along the sides of the path, without any gaps. This is what the Nukui widows were referring to when they talked about being able to escape from attacks by enemy planes here.

It is this path which was sown with the tears of the Nukui widows. It is also this path along which streams of casualties from Hiroshima fled, so that the bamboo thickets were once full of the dead and the injured. If you stop and peer into those deep bamboo thickets, shivers run up your spine and an eerie feeling comes over you.

Arriving at Nukui, you notice Seseragi Park, which was laid out between the old embankment path and the main road when the flood prevention work was carried out on the river. This park stands at a spot where the riverside used to be wide, and it was here that many atom bomb victims were cremated by their relatives over a period of about one month from 6 August 1945 onwards. There were even people who collected bones here and used them, after crushing them into powder, because they believed that human bones were effective in the treatment of burns. Chiyoko Sugita has said, 'if the ghosts of the victims of the atom bomb ever appear, it will be on the riverside at this spot', but I haven't heard any stories of people seeing ghosts. Standing there in the fullness of autumn, I could see that grass now covers the riverside sand, which was fertilised by the bones of the atom-bomb victims and watered by the tears of their families.

When you descend from the embankment path, you enter Nukui Village. It has been suburbanised now, with new houses and blocks of flats eating into the farmland, where they grow Hiroshima greens. The farming families still live in the old farmhouses and still work hard at growing vegetables. These families have their graves either in their garden or in a corner of a field close to the house. There is no cemetery here, so each house has its own established burial plot. Carved on the graves are phrases such as 'Resting together in peace' or 'family tomb', and on every grave what catches one's attention, along with words such as 'passed away', 'dead', 'deceased' and 'killed by the atom bomb', is the date '6 August 1945'.

Out of roughly 250 households in Nukui, altogether 198 people were killed by the atom bomb: 168 of these were in the National Volunteer Corps (86 men and 82 women), 18 were non-members of the Volunteer Corps, and 12 died from the after-effects of the atom bomb. Considering these figures, it is hardly surprising that there should be atom-bomb casualties in every family's burial plot. The victims were of all ages. They ranged widely, with 40 of the casualties being under 19 years of age, 44 being in their twenties, 31 in their thirties, 33 in their forties, 43 in their fifties, 1 in his sixties, and a further 6 being of uncertain age. From this we can see how merciless the atom bomb is as a weapon, when it massacres even non-combatants indiscriminately.

From 6 August 1945, Nukui was plunged into 'a hell for the dead and a hell for the living,' as Masako Nomura put it. Over the 36 years since then, it has re-established itself as a suburban, vegetable-producing district. In that peaceful, autumn village, every time I came across the grave of one of the atom-bomb victims, I clasped my hands in prayer, like a pilgrim.

It scares me, the way things are now

Hiroshima Municipal Kawauchi Primary School is located in Naka Nukui. At the time when the atom bomb was dropped, it was called Kawauchi National Elementary School and it was used as a collecting point for those injured by the atom bomb. Of the 150 people who were brought to this school, half died in agony and were cremated on the side of the River Furu.

In one corner of the school grounds, there is a monument 'commemorating victory in the three wars'. Carved on the monument are the names of 110 soldiers who fought in the three wars (the Sino-Japanese War of 1894–5, the Boxer Uprising of 1900 and the Russo-Japanese War of 1904–5). It was via these three wars that our country was led into the Pacific War. This monument witnessed the full horror of the atom bomb. Some of the injured might have fainted in agony even as they clung to it. Hence, I could not help thinking how hollow the words 'commemorating victory' looked against the background of the autumn sky.

To the left of the school gate, a stone monument has been erected 'for the repose of the souls of the military and civilian war casualties from Kawauchi Village'. It is a small, pyramid-shaped stone and was erected in December 1953 by the Kawauchi Village Widows' 'Shiraumekai' [White Plum Blossom Association]. Carved on it are the names of those who originated the idea – Chairwoman Chiyono Nishimura, Deputy-Chairwoman Haru Takasaki and Tomiko Fujii. I wonder what it is that the children can have leant by comparing these two monuments?

Nearly all the atom-bomb widows have said that their 'grand-children don't want to listen to what I tell them about the atom bomb'. Even so, with their personal experience of the atom bomb, they can't keep quiet, nor can they help wishing that 'even their children's children will never be involved in war'. Kiyono Fujioka's words come back to us here:

'When my great-grandchildren get to be 20, war could well break out and then the time might come again when people are killing each other. When I think about it, it scares me, the way things are going now. There mustn't be another war. There mustn't.'

But it is difficult for the children, playing in the school grounds, to understand the feelings of this old lady when she says 'it scares me, the way things are going now'. The atom-bomb widows sense a crisis in the present situation of suspicion that military expansion is under way and that nuclear weapons are being brought into the country. That is why they say 'it scares me, the way things are going now'. They desperately want to make their grandchildren, and the world at large, understand these things.

The life stories of 19 women

In July 1980, as the anniversary of the atom bomb approached, I had the idea of collecting the life histories of those atom-bomb widows whose whole lives have been spent on the land. Over the 35 years since the war, the memories of people's wartime experiences had been fading rapidly. Also, by then, those who had experienced the atom bomb were of advanced age. It struck me furthermore that there wasn't even a single coherent account of the impact of the atom bomb on farming women. I thought that if a record was not made now, there would never be any record of what the atom bomb did to the peasants. Thinking along those lines, the idea really took hold of me and, having selected Nukui, whenever I had a spare moment I would pay a visit to the atom-bomb widows.

I did not want to focus on the atom bomb alone. Instead, I decided to present the entire life stories of women who had lived through 70 or 80 years. I never asked them to tell me what happened when the atom bomb was dropped. Rather, I would get into conversation with them by asking them to tell me their life story, from the time they were born and, as a result, they told me their whole life story with great frankness. They showed me how the atom bomb, and the death of their husbands or their children, fitted into the pattern of their whole life as a woman, and how their way of living as a woman was altered. By so doing, the entire picture of the life which they had led up to now was brought into perspective. All of them, as they talked to me, unburdened their innermost feelings.

I never used a tape recorder. I do not like the idea of a machine intervening in a conversation between one human being and another. Instead, I conscientiously made notes of what they told me. In entrance porches, greenhouses, or wherever it was that the atom-

bomb widows would talk to me, I would plant myself down and
listen. Often I would use my knee as my writing table. Sometimes
after two or three hours' talking and taking notes, my fingers would
be numb. As I wrote everything down eagerly, so they would talk to
me with the same eagerness. Some of them would even adjust their
speed of talking if I got behind with writing my notes. I really entered
into the minds of those old grannies. I could feel myself breathing
their breath and shedding their tears. It did not worry me that
sometimes, as they talked to me, they would put the cart before the
horse, or their account would be somewhat tangled. From my notes,
I rewrote their accounts and put what they wanted to say into words.
In that sense, my record of their talks is not a simple, mechanical
reproduction of their conversation.

North of Kawauchi Primary School lie the Nukui Hachiman Shrine
and the Jōgyō Temple. I never asked anyone's permission, but
whenever I went to interview the widows, I always ate my lunch in
one or other of those places. When summer showers fell, I would
take shelter from the rain in the hall of worship of the Hachiman
Shrine.

The atom-bomb widows gather on the 6th of each month at the
Jōgyō Temple for a memorial service to mark the monthly anniversary
of the death of their husbands and children. They started this practice
soon after the end of the war, and still their monthly prayers are
continuing. During the first ten years after the war, more than 70
widows used to gather, but nowadays there are very often less than
20 of them.

In all, 26 atom-bomb widows are still alive and I could manage to
listen to the life stories of 19 of them. All of those I met are hard
workers. Whenever I went to see them, they would be out in the
fields. I would go along, thinking that I ought to find my interviewee
at home because it was a rainy day, only to discover the 84-year-old
granny out picking aubergines. Every one of them declared 'I hate
weeds' or 'Work is my life'. But if I visited them, they would stop
work and give up their time to talk to me endlessly. When I left,
they would press on me spinach, leeks, or – in the early autumn –
perhaps it would be *mouli* that they would pull out of the ground for
me. All of them were warm and kind-hearted old ladies.

As I stood in the deserted garden of Jōgyō Temple on 10 November
1981, this old lady and that old lady came to mind. Every one of
them had brought their talks to an end with remarks like: 'There
mustn't be another war' or 'They shouldn't make nuclear weapons'

or 'There's nothing crueller than the atom bomb'. These words of the atom-bomb widows could be said to be the final testimony of their life and I, for one, shall never forget them. We must never allow the memory to fade of what the atom bomb did in Hiroshima . . . Praying for the long life and peace of those living witnesses, I walked out through the gate of the Jōgyō Temple in the fullness of autumn.

Mikio Kanda
January 1982